Where The
Crazy People Swim

Outrageous goals, failure, and success

Steve Walker

All profits from *Where the Crazy People Swim* will be donated to Zanmi Lakay, a wonderful organization that helps street kids in Haiti, including providing teenagers with scholarships, meals for kids, computer and photography classes (using gently-used donated computers and cameras), and help in setting up businesses. The organization relies entirely on donations, and 100% of donated funds go to helping the kids.

Be successful and use it for good.

Cold-water ultra-marathon swimming is about as tough as it gets. The rankings in the sport are not determined by speed, but instead by which swims you finish. The hardest swims have only had a few or a few dozen finishers, often in hundreds of attempts. The answers to questions like, *how many miles? how cold was the water?* and *how bad were the jellyfish?* are qualifiers for the toughest swims. Failure is a possible (often likely) outcome in every swim, for every swimmer, but what doesn't kill you, makes you stronger.

Why would anyone take on something like the English Channel or the Irish Sea or any of the Oceans7? What drives a person to attempt to do something that they are very likely to fail at, and possibly even die attempting?

Where the Crazy People Swim lays bare the mind of a swimmer where he honestly and candidly describes his fears, his motivations, and his ultimate goal—not just in swimming, but in life. While covered by a veneer of swimming and honesty about failure both in the water and out, this book is about setting outrageous goals, and the definition of success.

Where the Crazy People Swim
By Steve Walker

Editor: Casie Finn
Proof Readers: Laura Gadola, Sue Walker, Scott Lautman

September 2016: First Edition

Contact the author: polarbearswims@hotmail.com

ISBN-13:978-1537573533
ISBN-10:1537573535

Dedicated to my parents, Annika, Kylie, and Ethan, and especially my wife, Sue. They inspire me to do cool things.

Contents

1 – Water 7
Failure 8
My First Real Swimming Memory 10
The Journey 11
2 – Choices 13
Cal 18
Quarter-Life Crisis 19
Dead Body 22
Doubting My Sanity 25
3 – The English Channel, 1996 29
Pre-Swim 32
Toward the North Sea 34
Toward the Atlantic 38
The Changing Tide 42
The Way Back to Dover 48
4 – Quitting Carbs 51
Diet 57
Bigger Picture 58
5 – The Split and Cobaltix 59
Back in the Pool 64
The Birth of Innovation Labs 65
Sue 68
Success 69
6 – Wild Sparks Extinguished 71
Swimming Goals 73
Goals, In General 76
Sleep 77
Stroke 78
Wild Sparks 81
7 – My Worst Fear Realized 83
Leading 85
Taking Risks 89
100-Year Goal 90
8 – Europe to Africa 95
Age 96
Gibraltar 101
9 – A Scare in Copenhagen 107
Hypothermia, Fat, Brown Fat, and Shunting 108
The Scary Swim in Copenhagen 114
10 – Irish Breakfast Is the Best 119
Ireland 121
Confluence 124
11 – Catalina 125
Learning and Growing 132

12 – Improving   133
  Tahoe   *134*
  A Few Cold Swims   *138*
  Co-Conspirator   *139*
13 – Failure, Juan de Fuca   141
  Chilling Out   *144*
  Damn Cold   *147*
14 – Ireland   153
  Windows and Pilots   *159*
  Cushendun, Cushendall, and Crew   *160*
  False Start   *162*
15 – Swimming The Irish Sea   169
  Greasing Up   *170*
  Cold Water   *172*
  Dizzy, Hallucinating   *173*
  Sprained Wrist   *177*
  Time and Mind Games   *178*
  Pain and Swearing   *181*
  Back on the Boat   *183*
16 – Those Who Finished and Didn't   187
  Analysis   *188*
  Is the Irish Sea Getting Easier?   *189*
  What Does It Take to Make It Across?   *191*
  What Is Next For Me?   *192*
  After the Swim   *193*
17 – The Last Word   195
  Ben Franklin   *196*
  Tell a Good Story Well   *196*
  Most Important   *196*
Appendix A – Feeding   201
  Water   *204*
  How Your Body Gets Glucose   *205*
  Insulin and Fat Metabolism   *207*
  Sugar   *210*
  Feeds   *212*
  Absorption, Osmolality, Glycemic Rate, Proteins   *220*
  Actually Feeding   *224*
Appendix B – Rankings and Big Swims   229
Appendix C – Planning a Swim   233
Appendix D – A Few Questions   239
Appendix E – Day and Night   247
Appendix F – What to Bring on a Swim   251

Aquatic Park from the South End Rowing Club

Acknowledgments

I am the weak link in this chain. I merely swim, and now am
writing a little about my swimming and my career, hopefully in
an interesting way. I learned early that it isn't what you do that
matters, but rather, it is who you surround yourself with and how
you help others.

I've managed to fall into incredible communities (both in swimming and business), and any successes you may read about here are theirs as much as mine. The failures are many and mine. I own them and try to learn from them, but the successes described in this book truly belong to the people who I've managed to entangle and ensnare in my diabolical schemes and plans.

<u>SERC and the Natadores Locos.</u> SERC is my church, and the Locos are my Sunday school classmates. At SERC, we break the rules. The Locos break the rules that haven't even been written yet.

Cam has been not only a great business partner, but also a great training partner. I'm very lucky that I have him. He's a great person both to train with and to work with. I couldn't ask for a nicer, more transparent, and completely modest person. Anything is possible with him.

Ranie got me back into the Bay after almost 15 years on the sidelines. She might be the most positive person I've ever met. Bill Wygant and Reptile truly represent the rule-breaking character of the club, even though they are the president and the swim commissioner. They make SERC what it is. Instead of kicking me out of the club for being a "rogue swimmer," they put together harder swims to help me train (Reptile's Nutcrackers). They are truly great guys, and I'm just one of the many people who have benefitted from their help.

Kim Chambers and I have marinated in the bay many days. She is an inspiring person and one of the most accomplished swimmers in our sport.

Capt. Mayhem may be the most rude and crass person I've ever met around the club (Stephanie completely makes up for him, though, and he's actually really normal when he's at work!), but somehow after a boat ride with him, you always feel like you can do anything. Although Les is wonderful (and is the only adult in the Mayhem-Kirk-Les triad), no one could ever match the power and warmth his lovely wife Sally brings to our swims. Kirk cannot be defeated.

Kelley has been a constant source of both positive energy and living evidence that anything is possible. Ryan, John, and Sofra are incredible guys to train with. I'm lucky they let an old guy try to keep up with them.

Bobby, Barry and the Irish mafia have made so many things possible (Barry sharing his locker with me, Bobby getting me my own locker, introducing me to Sarah, and both for introducing me to Ireland and helping me plan trips). I can't possibly ever thank them enough. Also, Amy is one of the nicest people I've ever met. She can swim forever and she's a great person to have on your crew at 3am! I will never be able to thank Joe and Dusty enough for piloting for me. They are both incredible guys.

There are many more people, too, who've swum with me and motivated me at SERC—Fran, Craig, Patty, Simon, Ron, Ashley, Darrin, Ed (Buster's best buddy), Mel, Bob, Laurie, Jim, Tina, Asha, Andrew, Victoria, Steve, Stevie Ray, Evan, Brooke, Vanessa, Kate, Melissa, Greg, Jeff, El Sharko, Al. I almost have to name everyone at the club. Also a few Dolphins as well, especially Larry and John. I feel bad, because I know I've left off more positive, wonderful swimmers than I could have possibly included.

Swimmers Around the World. Sarah has put me up at her house repeatedly and crewed for my Irish Sea swim. ("Don't worry about the temp, just get in and swim."). Modest and positive, she's just a great person in so many ways. Brian, likewise is an incredible person—so giving and kind. Keith put me up and trained with me in SF and Ireland, and introduced me to Oonagh, Ruth, Padraig, and Jacqueline—incredible people. Padraig is truly a steward of our sport and a great pilot. Likewise, Quinton is one of the best pilots I've ever had.

Andrew Malinak and Dan Simoneli are also both incredible stewards of open-water swimming. Their knowledge and encouragement have been incredibly valuable. Steve Munatones, likewise cares deeply about the sport, and his Oceans7 challenge and web site will live long after we are all gone. Scott Lautman and I have spent hours talking about how much fat is too much. He's an incredible athlete, an incredible steward, and an incredible guy. Scott Haskins and I wasted many hours talking about business while procrastinating on the beach in the 1990s (we've been friends for 20 years, and it all started with swimming). Donal Buckley is a scrupulously honest person who is a vast repository of knowledge about cold-water ultra-marathon swimming (and is a pretty accomplished swimmer himself).

For many of these people, the only way I'll ever be able to repay them is to pay it forward and help others in the sport we all love so much.

Work and Innovation Labs. At work, there are a few people who have helped me in ways that I could never measure. First Casie. She truly runs the entire company. The company would not be what it is without her.

Jay has been steadfast as both a friend and a colleague for 10 years. Through every possible success and setback, he's been there for me. Kerri has been an incredible source of pride for me. She came to the company as a consummate professional, and has only grown since then. She is always positive and brings great insight to everything that she does.

Andreea started a company at 22. She had every possible difficulty, and has overcome every single one. She is successful. I'm proud to have played even a small part in her success as a mentor, and know I will see her do things that will astound me.

Douglas has been a friend and he understands what I'm trying to do. He has introduced me to many of the interns and fellows, each of whom also deserves special thanks. I look forward to working with him for many years to come to do good things around the world.

Laura is a relative new-comer, but in a short period of time, she has descended on the company, and opened us up to thinking about things in new ways. She has been key to a lot happening at Innovation Labs, and likely will be for many years to come. For someone so young, she has incredible talent, and will do incredible things, both at the company, and in the world. She truly understands confluence. She will be a leader.

Finally, to Peter, Eric, Khalid, Wayne, Alex, Barbara, Rick, Mahboud, (and again my dad), and all those who have given me business advice (and even more, listened to me I'm sure endlessly at times), because I'll likely never be able to repay you, I hope to someday pay it forward in a similar manner.

Family and Friends. I appreciate my kids. We talk about swimming all the time, and they discount my talking (bragging), realizing that it is just fear and insecurity. They also have been truly interested and great listeners, indulging me as I work out what troubles my mind, long after others would have walked away. I'm very proud of them—each for different reasons. I truly respect and enjoy the people they are becoming.

My friends—Matt and Sam especially. Tiffany, and many others who have supported me both in business and swimming, every step along the way.

Likewise, my parents have never been anything but positive and encouraging. They taught me that anything is possible (even though my mom is afraid I'll be eaten by a shark). Also, I appreciate having such a successful and supportive family— Alicia, Buddy, Henry, and Terri (who all give me a ton of shit), and Ed and Christine (who are much nicer).

Finally, there is no way to even begin to thank my incredibly successful wife, Sue. Notwithstanding the love I have for her (and how beautiful she continues to be even as I get fat, bald, and old), I don't have words and can never begin to thank the person who is my partner in life and is the other half of my brain. She's made real sacrifices to let me go after these swims and my goals, no matter how outrageous. She is my biggest advocate and strongest support in swimming, business, and life. All my successes are because of her, and my deviations and missteps are almost always the result of me not listening to her.

Me, happy with good food; Paris 2014.

1 – Water

This is a story about a journey, not just a swimming journey. It is a story of failures—lots and lots of them. Failure is good. You don't always learn from wins. You never learn when you don't put yourself out there and take risks. There is an art to failing and it is necessary in success. Failure helps you understand what success is and appreciate it. Success is hard won, but the hard part is the failing. You need to be good at failing to be successful. You learn to stay positive.

At the end of the day, success is not a collection of things or accomplishments. It is about how much you help others. You can just donate money, or volunteer once a year at a soup kitchen, but success in life, what you want to be remembered by, what flashes by at the end of your life, will be much more. The impact your life has will be measured by how much you've touched others.

This is a story of confluence. Things coming together, reinforcing each other. It is also a story of starting things. Doing things when everyone says, "Are you crazy?"

Business, swimming, and that elusive end goal…they might seem unrelated, but not only are they related, they coalesce with each other, reinforce each other. The trick is understanding the end goal early enough in life to truly make a difference.

Failure

In technology and in business, you always want to know what is going to happen when things go wrong. Many people prepare by creating disaster recovery plans and having backups for all their major systems. They do mock DR failovers and test their backups quarterly, but somehow something else always fails, often catastrophically. Something always happens that wasn't supposed to happen.

You test a system by challenging it. You introduce things into the system that might cause it to break, ***often***. You push the system to the limits. You don't expect it to be perfect. You expect it to weather challenges. Lots of little failures are good.

You need confidence in the system to be real, not imagined and not false. The way to be sure systems (and also companies and you) don't fail is to tax them often. This introduces risk (something that people hate), but without this risk, there can be little real confidence.

This introduction of risk equates to doing new things. It means breaking systems. It means trying things that might not work. It means doing new jobs. It means being disruptive, innovative. You try lots of new things. Some things will fail. But a company (and a person) needs to fail (in small ways) often. There needs to be risk.

In ultra-marathon swimming, this equates to trying to do things that you aren't sure you can do. It means sometimes failing. You don't want to die, but you need to push yourself. It means trying new stroke mechanics (even if they "don't feel right"). It means trying new training techniques. It means going farther. It means being in colder water. Do things that surprise even you. And fail sometimes. Learn from failure.

In life, this means thinking out of the box. It means having an attitude of always saying yes. It means getting into trouble sometimes—not doing bad things, but not being afraid of looking stupid. It means doing things, even when you are busy or tired. It means being unafraid.

If you don't take risks, you aren't innovating. If you aren't failing, you aren't innovating. A company needs to be good at assessing risk, and recovering from failure. You need to be good at walking away from failures quickly—cutting them off before too much is invested in them. You also need to learn from your failures—that is the most important of all. You always have to be self-critical, as a person, as a swimmer, and as an organization. This is hard on confidence, but it is important.

We can learn lessons from the real world, and even biology. Kids that go to daycare (and are exposed to lots of germs, building up their immune systems), get sick less. When they do, they don't get as sick. What doesn't kill you, makes you stronger (literally).

The only way to truly be ready is to be constantly challenged. You want to fail in lots of small ways. You want to fail in a wide variety of ways. You want to press the limits of the system, so you know what your boundaries are. Those boundaries are probably a lot wider than anyone might think.

Look at the ways that things connect in your life.

My First Real Swimming Memory

The outdoors has been my religion my whole life, and the water my deity. It is more powerful than I am and on any given day, I do not know what it will let me achieve. As long as I understand that I can only control myself, I do ok.

My journey started when I was a little kid. I really wanted to swim. Always. When my dad's father died (he was in his early 40s and my dad was in his mid-20s), my dad's Uncle Ray and Aunt Caroline were there for him along with my Great Grandma Torkelson. This was all when I was little. We'd go up to Sacramento often, picking up Grandma Torkelson from her house on the way. It seemed like whenever I'd see her, swimming was involved. I wonder if that is part of the reason I so completely adored her.

I didn't know about why we were there, though. All I cared about was that they had a pool. One of my earliest memories was when I was about 5. We got up there late, and I was supposed to go to sleep. There were lots of adults awake, but all of us kids were supposed to be asleep. I really wanted to swim, though. I'd been talking about swimming all day, and when it started getting dark as we got close to Sacramento, I started begging to swim. Now I was in bed, I could see the pool through the window. I didn't sleep.

My parents came in after my brother and sister fell asleep, and told me to be especially quiet. They decked me out in Haldy's shorts (Haldy is my dad's cousin, but only a few years older than me). My Aunt Caroline got some string and made me a belt to hold them up. I swam. It was glorious. Not only was I swimming, but I was one of the adults.

In many ways, life has changed little since then for me, at least when it comes to swimming. I still love the water.

The Journey

This book is a part of my story. It starts just before high school, and goes through my attempt at the North Channel of the Irish Sea (one of the hardest swims in the world). It describes the sport of open-water swimming. There are some tips on doing cold-water ultra-marathon swims (which are probably only useful to me, and will be outdated by the time the book is printed). This is a story about swimming through the eyes of someone who loves the water.

The journey, though, is not just a swimming journey. It is also part of the journey I took in life, much of it centered around business. There are probably a few lessons—hopefully interesting. The journey has many failures, many setbacks, and many learning experiences and if I've chosen the stories well, one or two of the stories might make someone else's journey just a little bit easier.

I hope the stories in this book are interesting, but even more, I hope they are interesting to people who swim and to people who want to start and grow a company.

The book ends with my attempt at the North Channel, but that is not the end. The North Channel is the hardest swim in the Oceans7 (seven of the hardest swims in the world), which is my bigger goal. You'll have to finish the book or cheat and turn to the back to figure out if I made it to Scotland or not. I intend to do them all (and a cherry on top—a swim that I think no one else will be stupid enough to try), and failure will no doubt be a part of that journey. There is a great deal of risk involved (mostly personal risk—the risk of failure, and also a very small risk that I could die trying). On the business side, I have achieved some very cool things that most entrepreneurs only dream of, but I'm not done yet. I have a bigger goal that I'll tell you all about later in this book.

I have failed many times and I will fail many more times. It is a journey, and my ultimate goal is success, touching as many people in real ways as I can.

I ask people that I mentor one salient question (I wish I could attribute it, but I don't know who first asked it). That is, "What do you want it to say on your gravestone?" It often comes as a surprise to these young entrepreneurs, but you can't very well answer any other question until you know what you want out of life.

Hopefully by the end of the book, you'll understand how I answer that question, and how I intend to get there.

2 – Choices

What would cause a person to swim in freezing-cold water for hours on end?

A while back, a friend had asked me how long the English Channel took me to swim. When I told him, he said, "I can't even sleep that long."

There are people who I consider real athletes—Cal swimmers and water polo players for a start. All I have is some weird ability to stay reasonably warm in cold water and to just keep going for a long time. I know it is athletic, but also I know what real athletes look like (having a six pack and the swimmer's triangle back, for starters). I had the triangle, but never had the six-pack.

I swim well, although my stroke would never be used in a training film. My stroke is long and efficient. I get a lot from each pull. After 35+ years of swimming, I have a good feel for the water. I can also vary my stroke to the ocean conditions and to use different muscle groups when certain muscles get tired. It wasn't always like that though.

My parents were always my biggest supporters, especially academically. They quietly instilled a confidence in me that made it easy for me to take risks. Failure was always something that could be recovered from, something to learn from, and success in the bigger picture was always a question of how not whether or not it would happen. Also, setting very high goals and taking risks was just a part of the equation.

My parent's stories are theirs to tell, but their successes and even their failures formed me, and helped me understand what real confidence was.

My dad never hid his failures, and he set a very high bar for me. He was incredibly transparent, and showed me by example how fairness, honestly, being comfortable in one's skin were incredibly important, even if it took a long time to achieve the last. The lessons were there for me to learn.

My mom's genuine love of people and ability to climb into anyone's shoes helped me always see things from each person's point of view. My mom used to tell me that "the old lady that gives her last grain of rice is better than the one who takes out a checkbook." We saw this when we were little. We'd travel on a dime when we were young. Even having never seen the maids, my mom would always leave a generous pile of currency everywhere we stayed for them. It didn't matter whether we knew them, she said, because they had harder jobs than we'd ever know, and we had everything. It was the least we could do. As kids, we knew that leaving a little of our hard-earned money was part of traveling.

My parents put my dad through law school, and we were house-poor (they bought their first house when they were 24). When we were little kids we shopped for our clothes at second-hand stores and got hand-me-downs—they were perfectly good, and we'd outgrow them long before we wore them out. When I was about 13 everything changed. I know it didn't happen overnight, but it seemed that way when we moved to Lafayette. Funny, though, even though my parents had money when I was a teenager (and within a few years, a lot of money), as kids, it was never ours. They had nice cars and a nice house, and we starting taking fun vacations, but it was clear to all of us that we would have to earn our own money.

As a kid, I always liked swimming. When we moved to Lafayette, California in 1982, Mike Thornton (my 8th grade math teacher) convinced my parents that the three of us kids should be on the local swim team. At the time for us, that was LMYA. Mike was a great coach. He's responsible for me being a swimmer.

Immediately, I showed no talent for swimming except maybe the ability to not give up. I knew this because my sister, Alicia, was talented. She's 18 months younger than me, and she just kept getting better. By the end of the summer, she was faster than most of the girls on the team who'd been swimming since they were 6. She started swimming AAU (Amateur Athletic Union, now USS, United States Swimming) at Walnut Creek—the Aquabears. She broke all kinds of age group records, and ended up getting a full ride to Berkeley for swimming, eventually getting 6th at Olympic trials in the 100-meter butterfly.

That was not my experience. Mike was also my math teacher in 8th grade. He encouraged me to swim. No matter how hard people laughed as I thrashed the water, I kept trying. By the end of high school, I'd become an okay swimmer. I tried hard, but no matter how hard I worked, my times were never all that fast. Even at the longer events, I just seemed to have one speed—kind-of medium. I could do anything in practice, swimming for hours on end. US Nationals, though, was not a meet I would ever go to.

Mike encouraged me, though. He told me something that summer before high school that has stuck with me all these years. He said, "It is going to hurt. It is going to burn. It is going to be hard. If it isn't hard, you aren't trying hard enough." He ended up convincing me to play water polo at Acalanes, too.

Mike died young. He had a heart attack while I was a teenager. His wife was a famous swimmer (Karen Moe Thornton, former world record holder and Olympic gold medalist). She ended up coaching Alicia at Berkeley, and I ended up swimming Masters with her when I was in my 40s. Mike made a huge difference in my life. Mike gave unselfishly.

Anyone I've ever played water polo with could tell you that any skill I have is because I try hard—no natural talent at all, no shot. Sure, I'm left handed (which can be an advantage in ball sports) and I'm a strong swimmer. I've learned to be competent at the sport, too. I can't say I stood out in high school polo. I wasn't going to get any awards for my swimming either (except the most improved award once, and I think a coach's award), but I just kept trying. Even after 30 years of playing polo, all I have to show is a mastery of skills—still no real talent. I do like polo and like to play with good players, but I know that all I have is the ability to go for a long time and an ability to see how things are unfolding. I'm not the guy that scores the goals.

I had something funny happen to me in my senior year in high school. I was being recruited by Yale and Columbia. I was probably at about the right level academically, my grades and scores were solid. But East Coast schools weren't as good as West Coast schools in terms of swimming (there wasn't a lot of East Coast water polo at that point). I was good enough that I was being recruited at Yale and Columbia for swimming, but neither was a swimming powerhouse. Unfortunately, at a point in January, both coaches just stopped calling. When I called the Yale coach, he told me that he "couldn't help with ethics issues" and hung up. I had no idea what he was talking about, but I'd thought I'd done someone horribly wrong. I never called the Columbia coach. Needless to say, I didn't get in to either school.

In April 1986, I got into Berkeley. I wasn't talented enough to swim at Cal, but I was just stubborn enough to try. My sister was a year behind me, so I set a goal to make the team my freshman year. After that, if I wasn't fast enough, I could let it go, but I wanted to try.

I did eventually find out what happened with the other two schools. When I was applying for scholarships, I ended up with an extra copy of my transcript (a sealed envelope back in those days). I opened it. My high school had sent out the transcript of another kid with a name similar to mine, but he had a 2.1 GPA (mine was more in the A- range). That explained Columbia and Yale, and the other school I got rejected from.

I was pretty happy to be going to Berkeley. Except for the swimming (where I was out of my league), it was really where

I'd wanted to go since I was a little kid. My dad had gone there, and it was always the place I'd wanted to be.

Cal

I swam through my freshman year, barely holding on at every point. I was able to make it through the workouts, not easily but I worked really hard. I got better, especially at the 500 free, but I just wasn't in the same league as any of the other swimmers there. I'd be 158 lbs. on Monday morning, and 148 by Friday night. That was pretty much the whole season. I was stressing my body to the point of breaking every week, but without any real talent and my improvement would be within a range that was nowhere near everyone else on the team.

Matt Biondi was setting world records and we had Olympians from all over the world at Berkeley—17 of the 32 people on that team went to the Olympics for one country or another, a legacy that has carried on to the present day. Even the other "last guys" on the team had way more talent and faster times than me.

At the end of the season, I finished my collegiate swimming career. My fastest time in the 100 backstroke (my main event) had been a :58 that I did in practice. Paul Kingsman, who was a year ahead of me and has been a good friend ever since, went :47. That's a big difference. Funny, though, I did go 4:36 in the 500 free (again in practice). It was far off what the other guys were going (low 4:20s, and even a 4:19). Although I didn't realize it at the time, my 500 free was actually pretty quick. It took me a long time to figure out that it wasn't so much that I wasn't fast, it was more that I was running out of pool.

Still, although I'd made it through my freshman year and scored points for Berkeley in two meets (Cal Poly and Santa Barbara), I definitely felt like I'd failed. I got through my freshman year and grew a lot, but there was something missing after I stopped swimming competitively. I tried to substitute other sports (triathlons), but it just wasn't the same.

As my success or lack thereof in the pool was coming to an end, I was refocusing on school. Berkeley was teaching me a lot, but not about history. It was teaching me about who I wanted to be and what I wanted to become. I still hadn't decided what I wanted to be when I grew up...not career, and not who I was. I did know that I valued hard work, and that I wanted to provide more value than the pay I earned. I also realized that work was not the end goal; life was the end goal. I left Berkeley with more questions than answers, but at least I now had some questions. I also left Cal with a girlfriend, Sue, who I would eventually marry.

I did some triathlons while I was in college and just after I graduated. I found the longer they were the better I did and the more I liked them, even though I really didn't like the running. I coached swimming a couple of summers before I headed to DC for graduate school (leaving Sue in SF). While I was there, I played polo for an East Coast team called Rockville Montgomery (we even made it to US National, but were 12th of 12 by a long way, and I didn't even start). I also signed up for a swim across the Chesapeake. The weather meant that the swim didn't happen for me (it was delayed, and I couldn't wait it out), but it was my first inkling that there was a world of open-water swimming out there.

Quarter-Life Crisis

I say I had a quarter-life crisis (I think that's a real thing) when I turned 25. I hadn't accomplished anything. You might say that the English Channel and my success at work in my early 30s came out of that rough few months when I was 25. It makes a good one-line summary of that year, even if that is only part of the story.

My quarter-life crisis came after repeated failures. I went to graduate school in Washington, DC. I designed my own concentration (International Economics), wrote an excellent thesis (on the *Treuhand* and the German Takeover of East Germany after the fall of the wall) and (because Sue was still in San Francisco) I finished my coursework in 3 semesters. I didn't love DC. Everyone smoked and almost no one was athletic. The outdoors was something people talked about going to on vacation. Everyone seemed like they were in government or politics, there was no innovation and it was just plain depressing for me. I was pretty miserable, but this was not my quarter-life crisis. I weathered DC pretty well, and then I decided I was going to law school.

I came home, applied to law school, and (oops) didn't pass my graduate school exit exam. I have lots of excuses for not passing it (mainly, that I hadn't taken a single class from one of the three examiners), but at the end of the day, and to this day, I still don't have a Master's degree. Another failure.

I got into one law school, so I just pretended like the whole graduate school thing didn't happen. I'd had a job and had paid my way through school without any debt, so I just figured a law degree would make not getting my Master's degree moot.

I started law school (and was still working). My grades were ok, but I was surviving on a few hours of sleep each night. I hadn't yet figured out that I needed to sleep. Work was 40 hours a week, school was another 20 more, and studying was easily 60 hours a week. That left 48 a week for commuting, eating, sleeping, and (mostly not) working out. I'd usually study with Sue, killing two birds with one stone. At the end of the first year, my GPA was .003 below what was required, and I was put on probation. They wanted me to retake the class with the lowest grade. I wouldn't have to pay again for it, but I wasn't moving on with my class. Most people would call that a failure (another academic failure, too boot). I sure did.

It was about this time that I got a promotion at work, and I was loving technology. I loved the intellectual side of law school, but I hadn't gotten the hang of the writing (wasn't horrible, it just hadn't yet really clicked yet). I also realized that I wasn't ever going to practice law. I wanted to do technology.

I was not working out much (a few triathlons over the summers where I'd be in the top of the swim, done well in the bike, then hated every step of the run). I wasn't sleeping much. The only thing that was really working in my life was my girlfriend, Sue. And technology. I loved figuring out computers, the more complex the challenge, the better.

I decided to quit law school. (Not another failure, really just punctuating the previous failure where I was put on probation and didn't move ahead with my class.) So now, in the quest for letters after my name, I was officially a two-time loser. I decided to ask Sue to marry me. I never contemplated it at the time, but what a catch I must have looked like to her parents. She did say yes, but it didn't change things. I was still nowhere.

I was still in pretty great shape (even 5 years after hanging up my Cal suit). Running, though, was never my sport. I could do the runs (and could go a long way—36 miles was my longest run), but I just hated it, even though I did ok.

This was my quarter-life crisis. Two-time academic loser, and I hated my semi-adopted sport because of the running. I was at the bottom of the totem pole at work, and hadn't accomplished anything in life. No house. Wasn't even married.

Quitting law school and going full force into technology was my first real action as an adult, my first shot at being true to myself. It wasn't easy, but it was right. I knew it deep down. I had to move on if I wanted to be ultimately successful. I knew I would be, just not in school, not in law, and now, not at triathlons.

To say the least, my parents were not happy about me quitting law school. My mom couldn't even look at me without crying for months. She told me it was the biggest mistake I would ever make in my whole life. (She was quite wrong...I've made much bigger mistakes, since.)

I was suddenly about 80 hours a week lighter. I realized I needed something to do because even though work got better as a result of me quitting, I could only put an extra 20 or 30 hours a week into work. That still left me with a lot of time on my hands. I didn't drink, and was engaged. Partying had never been my thing anyway.

The time glut problem solved itself over a handful of weeks.

Dead Body

I was swimming at the "Y" in downtown San Francisco. I'd signed up to teach some inner-city kids how to swim. It was half altruistic. The other half was so I could swim there. It was a beautiful pool, right downtown.

I ran into an old friend from high school, Ken Hauser. He was the goalie at Miramonte High School when I was at Acalanes (he was a year ahead of me). We'd played summer polo together, but like most of the kids I'd played with, he was a lot better. Anyway, he talked me into swimming in the Bay the next day. I'd never done it before. I had no idea that there were people who actually swam in the Bay. I'd figured it'd be just the two of us.

He brought me down to the Dolphin Club. We swam on a beautiful sunny day in Aquatic Park with two quite attractive girls (they were 3-4 years older than us, and even though I was engaged, swimming next to good looking girls in swim suits still made the day that much nicer). I was still a very good swimmer (even fast by most standards), but the water was cold. We swam about a half mile. The route was called a round-trip flag—down and back along the beach. One of the girls (both of whom were also good swimmers) kept coming up short and stopping. When we got back, I asked her friend what was going on. She told me that this was her first time back in the water in a month. The last time she was in, she had run into a dead body—a Golden Gate jumper.

I was hooked. This was my sport! What other sport can boast water too cold to swim in, no walls or lane lines, beautiful scenery, and potentially running into dead bodies. They even had a sauna. I have always loved the sauna!

I'd never wanted to be part of a country club, but anyone could join the Dolphin Club (or the dirty, renegade club next-door— the South End Rowing Club, SERC). You just had to love swimming in open water. It was really out there. Who swims in 50-60F (10-15C) water (or colder) with dead bodies floating around? Me, that's who.

There were characters at the Dolphin Club in 1994. I didn't realize it at the time, but over the next 20 years, the Dolphin Club and the South End Club would go from being a figurative island where old guys (and women) swam in cold water, to one of the places that ushered in the sport of cold-water swimming, and help ultra-marathon swimming gain critical mass two decades later.

I quickly became friends with Scott Haskins. We're about the same age. We'd talk business waist deep in the water, procrastinating, sometimes for an hour. Then we'd swim for two, three, four hours—sometimes longer.

Susanne Heim had recently swum the English Channel. It seemed like a good goal. My time problem was resolving itself. If I was going to do this swimming thing and not law school, I was damn well going to do something worthwhile. The English Channel was as good as any goal. I had no idea how hard a journey I was embarking upon. I started reading. I read a lot. This was before the Internet (not actually before, but before the world wide web, web browsers, and the public Internet), so information was hard to come by. Scott was also training a lot. He was to do MIMS (the swim around Manhattan) that year. He also eventually did the other two swims in the Triple Crown—the English Channel and Catalina.

I trained a lot. Every day. Doubles. Night swims. Long swims. A ten-hour swim at 60F (15.5C) (20 miles/35km). I swam on the morning of my wedding day in August 1994 with my brother Henry (it was a great day). I swam through the winter. It got down to 48F (9C) that year. In the summer of 1995, I was in Australia (their winter) and I swam an hour at 42F (5.5C) in Melbourne (St. Kilda) at a very cool club there that had fencing underwater to keep the sharks out. A month later, I came back to St. Kilda and swam a mile at 37F (2.5C). The 37F (2.5C) swim would technically qualify as an ice mile (5C or colder), although it wasn't certified. This was long before "Ice Swimming" became a thing. I've never been too concerned with paper anyway. I did it for me, not for a piece of paper.

When I was in college swimming, I had trouble keeping my weight up. I had started shooting for 10,000 calories a day. It had worked, but I was always eating. I was always hungry, too—and also poor. I've been the same height since junior year in high school.

I'd decided 10,000 calories was the right amount for this, too. My typical meal was a baked potato for breakfast before swimming. After my morning swim, I'd stop and get a pint of Ben and Jerry's and four or five donuts to eat in the car on the way to work. At work, I'd have a pack of graham crackers, maybe a half dozen or a dozen of the little Reese's peanut butter cups, and 2 or 3 diet cokes. For lunch, I'd typically get a double bacon cheeseburger with a large fries. If they had strawberry shakes, I'd have a large one. Then I'd wash it down with a 20 oz. (550ml) diet coke. I didn't drink coffee, so the diet coke was my way of having a little caffeine (actually, probably a lot). I'd have more graham crackers and Reese's in the afternoon.

I'd usually swim doubles a couple of times each week. After work or swimming, I'd have a pretty normal dinner—meat, vegetables, potatoes/pasta/rice, and gravy. Portions were probably double what a normal person might eat, a whole day's worth of food for a normal person. By 9pm, I'd be back at the fridge. I'd have about half a half-gallon of coffee ice cream. Sue would have a little, then before bed, around 11pm, I'd finish the rest of the ice cream. We'd go through 4-5 half gallons (liters) of ice cream a week (not counting the Ben and Jerry's and we'd eat out once or twice a week). Lots of carbs and olive oil. Bacon was still a little pricey for every day, but buffets feared me. I didn't make 10,000 every day, but I did have a lot of fun trying.

Doubting My Sanity

I was putting in 25-40 cold-water miles (40-60km) a week—no pool. I'd had a couple of colds and that was worrying me, but I was swimming well. I'd made my 10-hour qualifier. I'd gone from my wedding weight of 192 lbs. (87 kg.), up to 243 (110 kg.), a gain of 51 lbs. (23 kg.).

As summer approached, I was feeling pretty good. There was just one problem. I seemed to be having trouble with longer swims—not the swimming part, but the approval part. The Dolphin Club really didn't seem to be behind me. Most of the members were, but there was always a negative element at the club, especially on the board. There still is. There was another woman attempting the channel (as it turned out, the same day), and she was having a little better luck getting pilots and permission for swims, but it was hard for her, too. Becky Fenson was a little faster than me and really nice. She'd swum at Michigan (she succeeded at the Channel the same day as I did).

By this time, I'm now 28. I'd gotten in trouble for doing one swim without permission (a non-club swim, where I jumped from the beach and returned to the beach) and another swim that I'd actually gotten permission for. I also seemed to be a target for those negative voices. Almost everyone in the club was 1000% behind me, but the few who were against made long training swims tough. I don't think it had anything to do with me personally, but the politics were just becoming a little too much for me. I just continued to weather it, and ignored most of it.

I started my taper in the middle of June. I felt terrible just like you always do when a taper starts. Sue and I headed off to England right after the 4th of July. I'd told people at work a couple of months earlier, and everyone was rooting for me.

My mom and dad were behind me, but my mom couldn't talk to me about it. She'd been very against me quitting law school and swimming with sharks wasn't much of an improvement. Sharks are not what you worry about. It is really about the cold and often jellyfish, but not in my mom's mind. She thought doing this whole computer thing was like doing construction. They both wanted me to make it to France, but they would have preferred that I was doing something that normal people do (like going to law school). They couldn't even watch.

It didn't help my cause when in June, I learned that a woman had died attempting to swim the Channel. I thought for quite some time it had been in 1996 that she died, but it turned out that the news reached me almost 8 years later (remember, no Internet yet).

I had to tell my parents (I probably should have not, but I was still pretty idealistic back then, thinking that perfect honesty was always best). Her death had scared me a bit, but the woman was skinny, and she was sponsored. She had advertisers in South America who would have abandoned her had she not finished. It was tragic. She never should have left Dover.

At this point, I had come a long way from where I was in college. I had a rudder, and I was starting to move forward, but I still only was starting to form an idea of where I was going, in my career and in swimming. I still didn't have any idea what my bigger goals were. I had a feeling that I was going in a direction that made sense, but it didn't seem sane. I knew simply making money or being very good at something was a stepping stone to something bigger, but at this point in my life, I didn't know what that bigger thing was.

Steve Walker

My Chart from the English Channel

3 – The English Channel, 1996

This is my journal of my English Channel swim. I wrote it almost completely in one night in Madrid, about 3 days after I completed the Channel.

It was Wednesday, July 17th at 8:30pm. I'd just gotten off the phone with Mike Oram. Mike was my pilot and the secretary of the Channel Swimming Association. As expected, I wouldn't be going Thursday, although it was likely that I would go Friday or Saturday. It was the day before the neap tide begins (the period between the full and new moon when the tides move the water less). It was also my mom's birthday. I tried to call, but I didn't get through.

I got in for about 45 minutes. Nice and easy. I saw Dieter. I felt very bad for him. Mike had told him that he would not make a Channel swim this summer. He was too skinny. Dieter is in his mid-forties, about 5'8", 150 lbs., and is about the same speed as me. He came from Australia.

Even though it would have been a possible day to swim, the wind was still blowing at about 15-20 knots. (One nautical mile is about 1.15 statute miles or about 1.85 kilometers. A knot is one nautical mile per hour, so 15-20 knots is about 16.5-22 mph, or 28-37km/hour. Wind around the world is measured in knots, so I'll stay consistent with that convention here.) The weather was better. Only a couple of days before, it was blowing 25-35 knots. It's unpredictable. Mike had said to hope for 10 knots.

I kept reminding myself of all the miles I'd swum to prepare: 90 miles (150km) in June, 350 miles (over 550km) in the last six months, 1,200 miles (nearly 2000km) in the last two years. I'd put in well over 2 million yards (nearly 2 million meters) in cold-water for this swim. I was ready.

On Thursday morning, Sue and I got up at 8am. We went down to the beach and I walked cautiously down the rocky beach (no sand), and hopped in for a 13-minute warm-up. Just getting wet and loose. The wind had died down some. It looked like Saturday would be the day. I wouldn't know until evening, though, after the weather report. The weather is on the BBC (TV1) at 6:30pm and 6:55pm.

After swimming, we got some food at a supermarket we discovered. Food in Dover is not ideal. Mostly fried or fast food. We also picked up a pole (the "feeding stick"), some clothespins, duct tape, the Channel grease I had ordered at Boots (kind of like Payless in the US), string, and an alarm clock to supplement my two watch alarms. We needed to get a feeding stick and string because I will be disqualified if I touch any person or the boat during my swim.

We did a little laundry (I couldn't believe that the matron of the launderette was smoking while we were doing our wash). I also picked up the cell phone for the gang to use in France to call the boat. After sleeping for an hour and a half and having some more carbs, we went back to the cell phone shop to get the cellular code for calling internationally.

The day seemed to go by quickly. There were many things to do before 5pm (when shops close) and 6:30pm (weather report).

At 6:50pm, I called Mike on the cell phone and he said the swim was a go for tomorrow at 3am. Robyn (my 13-year-old cousin) and the rest of the family (7 more cousins, aunts, and uncles) got back at about 7:30pm and everyone began getting ready for bed. Sue and I were down by about 9pm. Robyn and Sue are my support crew. Everyone else is hoping to meet us in France.

As I visualized the next day, this is what I contemplated:

> *Get down to the boat at 2am. Start around 3am. The tide will be washing me toward the North Sea from the start. Feed after the one-hour mark, then every 45 minutes until 5 hours. After that every 35 minutes. Take in a half bottle of warm Gatorade, and 1 Gu each*

feeding. Maintain 72 strokes per minute through the sugar rush, and the following insulin rush. Pee about every 20-25 minutes.

At about 5 hours, the tide should slacken for about 20 minutes. I should be done with 10 miles (16km) just under half way across. I should be able to see France if the weather is clear. After slack, the tide will begin carrying me toward the Atlantic. At around 10.5 hours, the tide will shift again. By this point, I should be nearing the coast, just south-east of Cap Gris Nez

When the tide changes, the current should push me straight into the Cap Gris Nez. If I am not at the coast by the time the tide changes (or shortly after), I will be washed back into the Channel. I may still be able to fight my way back to the coast, but it will take at least 3-4 hours.

Pre-Swim

I didn't really get to sleep until about 10:00pm or 10:30pm and I woke up slightly to look at the time 4 or 5 times in my 3 hours of real sleep.

At 1am, I heard Glenn (my uncle) stirring upstairs. I looked at the clock and decided to wait for the alarms, set to 1:10, 1:10, and 1:11am. At 1:05, Glenn came down and awoke us, afraid that we had turned off the alarms. He was as nervous as we were. By 1:40am, everybody was ready to go.

We drove down. It was ironic that people were still up at the time we were starting our day. We parked in the Hovercraft parking (24 hours for £3). Everyone else met up on the dock near the boat. We were right on time, but I joked that we didn't need to hurry, "What are they going to do, leave without me?"

Mike was preparing the boat, the Aegean Blue. Sue, Robyn, and I talked to everybody for about 15 or 20 minutes while Mike was getting ready.

I had started feeling nervous about 7 or 8 weeks before arriving in England—shortly after my 10-hour qualifying swim at the Dolphin Club in the San Francisco Bay. I went nearly 22 miles (32km) that day, but toward the end, I started getting cold. After feeling cold in my longest practice swim, I worked hard to gain another 10 lbs. (5kg.) on top of the 15 (7 kg.) extra I already had. I was also thinking that the water would be three or four degrees (about 2C) warmer in the Channel than in the Bay at this time of year. Actually imagining swimming was inciting the butterflies to stir. In San Francisco, I was able to laugh it off as "still a ways off." Not now.

When I was buying the alarm clock, it hit me. "This is the last thing to do. No more practice; no more work; no more talking about it; no more diet; no more weight gain; no more plans; no more predicting, pacing, or timing; no more time." The day before the swim was calm. I knew I was going before seeing the weather, before talking to Mike. I was nervous. I snapped at Sue a couple of times. Was the weather going to be perfect?

It was too late. I was surprised by my alertness, my calm. I talked to everybody a little. I was even humorous, although a bit quiet for me. We pushed off for Shakespeare Beach (just west of Dover) and waved good-bye to everybody. I decided to wear my watch. I wanted to know how far I had come, even if Mike wouldn't tell me. The decision to wear my wedding ring was easy, I hadn't taken it off in two years. I couldn't have gotten it off anyway. Thinking about my extra pounds made me smile— added insurance. I decided to wear my small, lycra suit this morning. I chose it over my larger, new, nylon suit. I'm not sure whether the larger, nylon suit would keep me warmer by covering more of me. I opted for less drag. I didn't think that either one would make any difference.

I took off my shirt. Sue put the Channel grease on me. I didn't want a lot, just on my left shoulder (to protect my shoulder from the rub of my beard), on the back of my neck (cap rub), and on my underarms (lat rubbing). Sue also put on a ton of Bullfrog SPF 36—on my back, neck, ears, nose, cheeks, and forehead. When we got, close, Mike gave me a fluorescent green light stick (about two inches long), shaking it and saying that it would last 12 hours. Sue pinned it on my suit through the string in back.

As we approached the shore (about 40 feet/12m away), I put on my cap. I took 2 minutes of nervous procrastination and dove in. I fixed my cap and goggles for the last time and swam in to the shore. Mike yelled to go, and I started down the rocky shore and into the water. I realized after I had waded in, that I hadn't even felt the rocks on my feet. I left Dover at 2:50am.

Toward the North Sea

The pre-dawn colors were beautiful. The pink of the dawn contrasted with the dark blue of the water and the grey sky to the west. Very serene. Unfortunately, the first few hours of the swim were not serene.

After walking down the beach (the rocks, actually), I swam quickly to the starboard of the boat and it began following me. Within about 15 minutes I began to have three problems that I dealt with throughout the journey: high waves, exhaust from the boat, and the lateral wash of the tides.

The waves were bad within the first mile. There wasn't much wind in the first two hours. At least I didn't see any white horses (white caps) or feel any spray on my face. The tidal waves, however, were high—four to six feet. The waves themselves weren't the main problem; the difficulty was that I couldn't see them coming.

In addition, because I was on the starboard side of the boat, the waves coming down the Channel (with the tide) hit the boat first. This was supposed to reduce the waves hitting me. As each wave hit the boat, though, the boat rocked to absorb the wave, which in turn created another wave (or waves), which were out of sync with the water underneath the surface. Result: Steve tossed around like a rag doll.

It was difficult to choose when to be stiff (to keep the best form and maximize my stroke) and when to be limp (to absorb the energy of the wave). With synchronized waves, it's possible to "snake" the waves to keep from losing ground. But with these waves, many strokes find no water and many times a breath meant a big swallow of water. The Channel is very salty.

I swallowed a lot of water in the first couple of hours. I estimated about 4 oz. each time, probably 8 or 9 times an hour. The waves crashing on my head gave me a headache. The combination of the waves and the exhaust left me feeling pretty crummy—no seasickness, but serious irritability, and swelling in my throat from the salt water.

Aside from the actual swimming speed and the time for stops, the next most important factor is precise navigation. Precise navigation is very difficult with the waves. Not only are the waves disorienting, but the tide pushes the boat laterally at a different rate making navigation hard for Mike.

Forty minutes into the swim, I yelled at each breath "Feed...Five...Minutes." Sue and Robyn weren't nearly ready. The feed lasted more than 2 minutes. That was 1.5 minutes longer than I'd planned. The Gatorade was not warm, and the bottle wasn't on the string. I had to get it back into the boat wasting valuable time and energy. Also the boat didn't stop all the way. I was pissed.

I learned after the swim that Sue had been sick five times in the first two hours. After the swim, I also found out that our other passenger, who was training to be a Channel Swimming Association official observer, had also gotten sick repeatedly. He is employed as Ferry Boat Captain.

After not being ready for the first unscheduled feed, both Sue and Robyn performed perfectly on every single feeding thereafter. My next feed was 35 minutes later. The Gu didn't taste right. I wasn't getting any boost in energy.

The waves continued to be very rough. I realized that the exhaust pipe had a leak at mid-ship on the starboard side and that during the first 2 hours I had sucked in a lot of fumes.

At about 2 hours, I yelled to the boat to have Mike stay behind me so that I could "lead" the boat. I wanted to be able to see the waves and avoid the exhaust. At about 2 hours and 20 minutes, I yelled again for Mike to stay behind me. Mike stopped the boat. I yelled again for him to follow me. He shouted, almost enraged, "Are you swimming back to fucking Dover?" as he pointed straight ahead to the lights of the Dover harbor. He continued, "How the fuck can you follow me if you're in front of the boat? You're swimming in every direction but up your own asshole." He then asked me if I wanted to switch sides. I realized that he was right. Although I hadn't told anyone about the fumes, he knew. He said that the fumes would be blowing away from me on the other side.

Switching sides helped a lot. When I was swimming ahead of the boat, the tide was carrying me laterally away, and I was dragging us off course.

I began swimming straight, looking right in a kind of water-polo semi-heads-up pattern. Every three strokes I would get a good look at the boat. I became quite used to the breathing pattern within just a few minutes, but I know that it was not as fast. Trying to avoid sailboats and buoys in the Bay had been good practice. I was still swallowing water, but my head cleared up without the exhaust. I estimated that I probably only covered 3 miles (5km) in the first 2.5 hours.

Through the second two hours, I fed about every 25-30 minutes. I signaled feeding breaks, rather than waiting for Sue. This worked ok, though, because I got both dehydrated and hypoglycemic a lot sooner than I expected. At about 3.5 hours, I asked for a half PowerBar at the next break. I don't think that my stomach handled the Gu very well in the first few hours. I'm not sure whether it was being caused by all the salt water that I had swallowed, or by the carbon monoxide and carbon dioxide in my blood from the exhaust. I needed to have something that wouldn't go into my bloodstream so fast.

I contemplated stopping and trying again in a few days. I reasoned that the waves would be smaller. But if I were to stop now in the hope of better weather, I would have to give myself at least five or six days to recover. At the end of the neap tide (shortly before the moon was full) the weather might be as bad as or worse than today. I decided to press on.

Shortly after 4 hours, Robyn clothespinned a half-PowerBar onto the end of the stick. I couldn't discern the flavor, but it didn't matter. I just needed to get more glucose to my muscles. It felt good. This was the first of 4 half-PowerBar feedings, which lasted 2-6 minutes each (because of chewing, mostly), and my stroke count dropped from about 70 per minute (during the first four hours) to about 56 per minute. I figured that my overall speed probably took a hit, too, although I felt like I was pulling more water with each pull. The PowerBars are harder to digest, have more calories, and have more sugar. At the feeding shortly after 6 hours, Sue only offered me Gu, and told me to try to last longer; my feedings had been too close together and too long. At least I got in 8 oz. of full strength Gatorade at about 140 degrees (about 65-70 calories) at every feeding.

Toward the Atlantic

We saw the best conditions between 5.5 hours and 6 hours. I guessed that the tide went slack then. The tide began to carry me toward the Atlantic. I had struggled with the high waves for about 5.5 hours, but it seemed as though the worst was over. I knew that I had lost a lot of time, but at least the waves now were easier to handle (1-3 feet, or <1m). I remember thinking that I might be able to make up some time.

At the feeding at 6 hours, I dared to ask where I was. Sue would give me an indication at the next feeding. At about 6.5 hours, my 13th feeding, Sue told me where I was. I had only covered 8 or maybe 8.5 miles (about 13km). I knew immediately that this was not a good thing.

Over the next half hour, I did some figuring. Sue told me that my pace had been about 1.5 mph (2.4km/hour) over the first 5.5 hours, and that it had increased to about 1.7 mph (2.7km/hour) between 5.5 and 6.5 hours. I knew that I should have been going at least 2 mph (3.2km/hr). I was almost 2 hours behind schedule. I had anticipated covering 12 miles (19km) by 6.5 hours, but I had only covered 8.5 miles (13.5km). Now, even if I increased my speed, I would not be able to hit Cap Gris Nez on the ebb tide, and the tide would carry me back out into the Channel. Only a small percentage of swimmers who miss Cap Gris Nez make it to French soil.

I figured that I would be in the water for between two and four hours past Cap Gris Nez. Could I still make it? At my feeding at about 7 hours, Sue told me that Mike had set a new course to account for the trouble we had had in the first five hours. I realized that the new course would not help me make Cap Gris Nez. The tide would change without me in less than 4 hours, and I still needed to go another 11 more miles (18km). At 1.5 knot pace, it would take me another 7 more hours.

I wouldn't make it. Could I handle 12-14 hours, another 5 to 7 more hours? I quit. I gave up. I stopped. I did some backstroke and breaststroke. My arms were wasted. My lumbars and abdominal muscles were aching. My throat hurt. I swam breaststroke over to the boat. Sue knew that I had just fed. The insulin rush might have contributed to my giving up. Sue told Mike and Norman (Norman Trusty, the Channel Swimming Association official observer) to get outside because I was coming to the back of the boat.

I didn't grab the ladder. Partly because I was too tired to lift my arms; partly because I could not bear the thought of failure, even though my body had already reconciled itself to it. Norman was out first. He said, "Steve, if you do this now, you'll never, ever have to get into cold-water again." He said some other things, but they blurred together as though Mike and he were one voice. I was kind of delirious from fatigue by this point.

Mike said, "Steve, this is just your body beginning to convert its fat to fuel. It's bloody well going to hurt. Every swimmer that finishes the Channel wants to get out at about 8 hours. If you can talk to me to say that you want to get out, you can still keep swimming. Now get back out there." Norman added, pointing, "You can see France. You're a little behind, but you'll make it." I couldn't see France over the waves, but it didn't make any difference. I realized that my body was not only burning fat as

Mike had said, but it was also beginning to metabolize muscle as well.

I began swimming. Mike was right, it did hurt.

After Norman and Mike's lecture, my pace moved to 1.8 mph (3.0km/hr). On my next four feedings, I only drank Gatorade, and each stop was less than 30 seconds. I didn't realize it at the time, but Norman was not only the observer, but also had failed to cross three times, before making three successful crossings in his late 40s. He and Mike were now both in their early 50s.

At about 8 hours and 20 minutes, I began seeing jellyfish. Because visibility was poor, I could only see about 8 -10 inches (20-25 cm). I couldn't see my hands underwater as I was swimming. But the "jellies" were "lit." They appeared to be about 2 feet below the surface, more or less. I estimated that there were about 200-250 jellyfish over about 500 yards/meters. I sidestepped 4 or 5 that were shallow, perhaps overcautiously. They were about 6-10 inches (15-25 cm) in diameter, 2-5 inches (6-12 cm) deep, and round like thick pancakes (not spherical). The outside was clear; the middle was bright, fluorescent blue. Some had blue leaking out toward their edges (tentacles, maybe). On those that the blue was leaking out, the middle blue was fainter.

I almost wanted to get stung, but only on my feet, not my arms, hands, or face. I doubt any one could have caused too much pain; maybe a few stings would even warm me up. A lot, though could end the swim. I avoided them. It would have been terrible to have stopped because of hundreds of jellyfish stings, after I had already decided at 7 hours and 10 minutes to finish no matter what.

At about 9 hours, I moved back onto the starboard side of the boat for about 1.5 hours to help ease the strain on my neck. I knew where the leak was and I avoided being near it. My pace on the starboard was about 2.1 mph (3.4km/hour). From the time I stopped until 10.5 hours, my pace was steady, between 1.8 and 2.0 mph (mostly at 2.0). The lateral wash from the tide was still challenging on both sides of the boat. The boat can't go slower than 2.3 mph (3.7km/hour) and still maintain its course. I worked out a pattern of leapfrogging the boat. I would swim up alongside the boat to the front then let the tide wash me away from the boat, letting the boat pass me, swimming back toward the boat, and up alongside it again. This way the boat could navigate, too. Each leapfrog took about 8 to 10 minutes.

I had noticed that Robyn had fallen asleep for a few feedings, but she was back up again. Sue did not miss a single feeding. They were great—always positive, totally even and level-headed, even when things were not so good. Starting at about 9 hours, my feedings got to be more regular. Each of these came about every 4-45 minutes, lasted less than 1 minute, and consisted of 1 Gu, and 8 oz. of Gatorade. I digested these without difficulty. These five feedings were the only "normal" feedings.

At about 9.5 hours, the tide went slack again, but at the same time the wind picked up to force 5-6 (about 25 mph or 40km/hour). The waves had been about 1-3 feet (<1m) since the tide shifted the first time (at 5.5 hours), but they rose to 6 to 10 feet (2-3.5m) at about 8.5 hours. It was easy to determine the size of the waves, especially in the light. I swam 10-30 feet (3-10m) from the boat and watched the boat being lifted as high as 12 feet (4m) over my head (twice my height). The later waves (after 8.5 hours) were much less predictable than the bad waves had been at the beginning but I had a few advantages here, though:

1. I was going to finish and could faintly make out the France
2. It was light out

3. It was sunny
4. I was able to see the waves coming and was not breathing in exhaust fumes

The sun helped a lot, if not in reality, at least psychologically. Even with everything in my favor, I was still swimming through higher waves than I had ever experienced in my life. I paid for my decision to continue. At 7.5 hours, I was thinking, "OK, but I might need surgery on my shoulders." By 9.5 hours, I was pretty sure that I would need surgery. I felt like I had saved up $20,000 and now was writing one big check. A lot like buying the house. All of a sudden, the account balance is $79.54.

At 10 hours, I stopped for my feeding, and something was weird. Everything on the boat was normal, but I glanced around. France had white cliffs, too. Sue had told me before we left that the White Cliffs of Dover existed in France, too, but I had not believed her. My feeding was unremarkable other than...*I was looking at Cap Gris Nez!* I was less than 1 mile from France. I couldn't understand why everyone on the boat was not as excited as I was. We were looking at 500-foot (150m) cliffs from less than 1 mile (1500m) away. Had I increased my speed that much?

No one had to tell me, but Sue and Norman relayed to me what I was already realizing. I was within 1 mile (1500m) of France, but the tide was turning. They told me to get on the other side of the boat so that it didn't run me down. Within 10 minutes, I lost sight of Cap Gris Nez. I never saw it again from that close.

The Changing Tide

The tide changed quickly and for the first time, I could feel it moving me. I was on my way North and East up the Channel to

Calais (pronounced "Cal-ee" by the British). I swam hard for about an hour, straight toward shore, but I realized later that I was only moving at about 400 yards (360m) per hour—less than 1/8 of the pace I had been holding. My stroke rate was a nice, even 72. From 10 hours until 11 hours, my pull was pretty good, but I was swimming straight at shore, but moving at 2 knots up the coast. I thought that I was still going to land on the other side of Cap Gris Nez because I was just swimming as hard as I could.

During the first 7 hours, I peed about every ten minutes, mostly because of all the salt water I had swallowed. It was very hard to pee, not like in the Bay. It would take between 1-2 minutes to finish, and the first 3/4 of that time was spent in a dead man's float, not moving at all. (I think this scared Sue and Robyn the first time, until they realized what was going on.) In my training, I had it down to 15 seconds. After 7 hours, I was peeing every 20-25 minutes and only stopping for a little over a minute, although it was still hard. I think that the extra effort was a result of my muscles being much tighter from having to absorb the waves. All the peeing probably added more than 40 minutes onto my time, almost 25 minutes more than I expected.

At my 10 ½-hour feed, I asked for chocolate. Thinking that I was less than 2 hours from the end, I asked again. I asked again at 11 hours and 15 minutes. Sue said no again. I told her nicely to get it for me. She would not. She knew. I didn't. Had she given me the chocolate at this feeding and at each one after it, I would have bonked after 2 hours—1 hour from finishing. Even though my muscles and liver could have soaked up the excess sugar as it came in, by the fourth feed of nearly 200 calories of pure glucose, my body would have begun producing insulin to counteract the high level of sugar in my bloodstream. This would have resulted in a bonk much like what happened at 7 hours, only much worse.

What would have happened: After seeing an initial increase in my stroke rate as a result of the first sugar rush, my stroke rate would have diminished significantly, as would have my distance per stroke. By the fourth feed of candy the insulin rushes would have become much more pronounced. During intense exercise, the body might be caught off guard by the first high dose of glucose, but it will react more and more strongly, flooding the circulatory system with insulin with even a small intake of glucose. My brain would have been left with little glucose and as a result I would have become unfocused, probably even dizzy and disoriented. My body then would have begun breaking down fat, but by the time enough had been released, I would have been finished. As a result of the decrease in my energy output, I would have begun producing less heat. This heat, which had protected me from the cold all the way across would have given way to the 59F (15C) water, and within 5 to 10 minutes, I would have lost more than 3F (2C) of body heat and shivering would have begun. Another 5 minutes in this extremely fatigued state and I would have had to have been pulled from of the water, shivering uncontrollably, unable to comprehend anything being said to me, or even where I was.

Sue knew.

Cap Gris Nez had long since disappeared. I was close, within 1 mile (1500m) of shore. Either Mike or Norman said that I could float in, but to keep going hard so that I could finish sooner. I preferred to float in, as he stipulated I could, but I accepted his advice. At about 11 hours, with no power left in my wet noodle arms (moving at about 76 strokes per minute), I began an eight beat kick. I continued this kick for 2.5 hours.

My feedings were still at about 45 minutes. Gu and drink, less than 50 seconds. Good.

During the weeks preceding the swim, Sue had read Paul Jagasich's *The Two Faces of the English Channel*, and Penny Dean's *Long Distance Swimming*. Both said to have some questions that swimmer could answer with little thought, but not from memory (e.g. "What airline did you fly to England on?", but not "What is your phone number?"). This is to help determine the body temperature—but it is imperfect as the level of fatigue must also be taken into account.

I asked Sue to give me capitals. From the first break, I had given her state or country capitals before she could ask for them. At 3 hours, I stopped because the breaks were taking too long, and I was a little stressed. At 8 hours, after Mike told me he would not take me back on the boat, I began again with the capitals. It was a sign that I would be all right. I stopped after that because I wanted to have shorter breaks. At 12 hours, I gave them Sao Paulo, Managua, and Quito (KEE-TOW!!!). After I'd taken down my Gatorade, I told them that they had better take me out, because Brasilia is the capital of Brazil, not Sao Paulo.

At 12 hours and 45 minutes, I was at what was to be my last feeding. I could actually see some progress. A sailboat passed closely in front of us. Mike brought the boat very close to me and sounded his siren. I had heard the siren about 25 times during the course of the swim, mostly in the first 5 hours. It meant that I was too far from the boat. I hated hearing it more than hearing the sound of a dentist's drill.

From the point that I lost Cap Gris Nez until about 13 hours and 5 minutes all I was doing was spinning my arms and kicking my legs. At 13 hours and 5 minutes, I felt it. I stopped. I almost cried. I thought to yell, but I couldn't. My throat was too swollen to even talk. I peed quickly. The waves died down at that instant. I had felt the thermocline. I was at the coast. The bottom had just come up from 40 meters to 10 meters. The temperature had just jumped to about 70F (20C+). It had been 59F (15C) the entire way to that point.

It was at this point that I knew I was actually going to make it. I looked at France, and I was 300 yards/meters out. I was being carried up the coast toward Calais. I put it into gear. My arms were spinning at about 80 strokes per minute, and I was kicking a kickboard sprint. I went for 20 minutes like this until Mike came on the loud speaker saying, "I have to stop here, it's only 5 feet (2m) deep. Swim ashore, get out all the way, pick up your rock, and get back here. Don't stop on shore, you'll get cold."

Sure enough, 25 yards (25m) later, I hit bottom—about 3.5 feet (1m) deep. Another 25 yards (25m) and I began pushing off the bottom. Another 20 yards (20m) and it was only 2 feet (less than 1m) deep. I started crawling. Finally, it was only one foot (35 cm) deep. I would have to stand up. I didn't fall, although I felt like I might.

A Frenchman, about 25 or 26, wearing a red shirt, had been watching me. While the surf was still at my feet, he said something and reached out to shake my hand. As best as I could, I raised one finger and tried to say "moment," but nothing came out. I took three hasty steps toward the beach. On dry sand, I turned to him and extended my hand. Five seconds earlier, he had asked me in English, "Did you come all the way across?" It finally registered and I answered him with a nod and a smile. Both raising my hand and smiling were very painful. He said, "Congratulations." His girlfriend walked up (she was wearing a white shirt). She said something that did not register. I shook her hand also, and whispered a very strained, "Thank you." I was glad that I had thought to not let him shake my hand, because it would have disqualified my swim. I gave them the international cold/shiver sign (actually it was real, the wind was very chilling on my wet, prune-like body). I began walking back to the water. I raised both arms (barely) back to the boat in victory, and when the water was back up to my knees, I crumpled into the water and began letting the tide carry be back out to 5 feet (2m) deep, where the boat could pick me up.

I realized then just what I had been up against. Clutching the small rock I had picked up, I was being carried at about 2.3 mph (3.7km/hour) toward Calais and back out toward the middle of the Channel almost as quickly. I did grab a rock, not a shell. I did exactly as I was told. In my dazed state, I didn't know if it was tradition or for some official purpose.

I had long since given up any thought that any of my family would be on the shore to meet me. I knew that I was not near Cap Gris Nez. I found out later that I had been carried past the town of Wissant (pronounced "Wesson" by the British)—more than 6 miles (10km) up the coast from Cap Gris Nez. Looking back at the beach one last time before going back to the boat, what did I see but Katie and Erika running furiously toward me along the beach. They told me that they had been chasing me for 6 miles (10km), watching the boat being carried by the current. Barbara came up a minute or two later, followed by Kristopher and Betsy a few minutes behind. They took some pictures, and we talked, me shouting barely audibly with the last of my voice. It was great to see them. I started to get very cold. About 10 minutes after I landed, I began making my way back to the boat, slowly.

Mike brought the boat in to 5-foot (2m) depth, not using sonar now, but by watching me on the bottom. I was about 100 yards (100m) from the shore now. I don't remember much about getting on the boat, but I do remember not being able grasp the rail on the ladder and hooking my arms around the rails at my elbows. I remember Robyn putting towels on my head, shoulders, neck, and waist. I remember Norman putting a wool (scratchy) blanket on me, and Sue giving me some hot Gatorade (about 190 degrees, 90C). It was so good. I asked for a PowerBar and some chocolate, and she had them for me before I had taken a step.

The boat was already moving. Although I was stable, and not overly cold, I asked to sit down inside. Robyn started to bundle me up and Sue wiped the grease off me. It came off easily. Sue had to go in and out because she didn't want to get sick. I ate and drank, and thanked Mike and Norman for talking me into staying in near the middle. Robyn dried my hair. Sue put stuff away and took off the light stick. They got me into my sweats and put on my parka. I didn't have enough strength to dress myself. I also asked Robyn to put two pairs of socks on me. Sue gave me 2 Aleve and a Cadbury Caramel.

The Way Back to Dover

I climbed tentatively down the stairs into the sleeping quarters on the boat, now completely unable to talk and not able to stand upright without help. Sue put me into the sleeping bag. I am falling asleep. My mind is racing, but my body is in need of sleep.

My throat is sore and swollen. It is difficult to breathe. My tonsils are the swollen and feel like a raw pork chop in the back of my throat and I have repeatedly, mistakenly tried to swallow it. My nasal passages are swollen shut. I didn't get any water in my eyes (I only took off my goggles once and only just to relieve the pressure). Still, I am blind to anything farther than an arms-length away inside the boat (like snow blindness). My lips are severely swollen. I am breathing at 35 breaths/minute, fast but solid. My heartrate is 70-75 lying down, 90-95 standing up.

My fingers are extremely pruny and completely white, (except places that had calluses—those places show pink scar tissue). I cannot touch any finger to any other, nor touch my thumb to any finger. My extenders and flexors in my forearms, as well as my metacarpal and thumb muscles are extremely swollen and are causing a great deal of pain, although I am sure they would recover.

My trapezius, lumbars, and abdominals are sore to the point that it is difficult to keep my balance—they aren't holding my weight anymore. My biceps, triceps, lats, quads, and calves are very sore, but only sore, not damaged. They will be fine. My deltoids are damaged. The next week or month will determine whether the damage has caused scarring in the ligaments and tendons around and connecting to the deltoid, or merely damage and/or scarring of the muscle which won't require surgery. There is a great deal of "bad" pain whenever I lift my arms.

I am not particularly sunburned and, except for one raspberry on each side of my suit on my upper-inner thigh (from rubbing my suit), I am pretty much free from any cuts, burns, or abrasions.

I slept for about 2 hours, waking with a brook of slobber running down my arm. My right arm is slightly cold, as I had been sleeping on it. My feet are like ice (dumb move Steve, putting two pairs of socks on to shunt all the warm blood away).

I went to the bathroom (very difficult). My throat is still bad and it hurts to breathe. Mike said that I should have brought mouthwash. (Betsy, my aunt and a neuro-trauma nurse told me that alcohol aids evaporation and would reduce swelling.) Since I didn't bring any, Mike gave me Extra gum. (Again Betsy: Extra has mannitol for that "cooool" feeling. Mannitol is used to reduce the brain swelling in head trauma cases.) We got back shortly after I awoke, and we thanked Mike and Norman.

I realized that I hadn't gotten my passport stamped. :)

Postscript

I woke the next morning at 7:30, but by 3:00, I began fading and needed to sleep. Each day after that I got a little stronger. It took about five days before I really felt ok. I rested my shoulders for two weeks before swimming again. They hurt a great deal but did not require surgery. My throat was sore for five days. The first three days after the swim, I could only eat ice cream without excruciating pain. During the swim, I lost 12 lbs. I estimate 6 of that to have been water loss. Three days later, I had gained all but two lbs. back. As of August 7th, I had lost 10 of the 25 extra lbs. I had gained in the months leading up to the swim.

I got back in the water. It was cold.

4 – Quitting Carbs

After I got back, I had a hard time. I put a lot of time back into work. Sue and I were both working hard.

I had a hard time explaining what I had done when people asked. Most people just didn't get it. A lot of people wanted to hear about it, but I didn't have a good way to communicate something so big with people. It had been cold. It had been miserable. It had been hard. Painful. Difficult. It was pretty huge, though.

Psychologically, I was empty. I put a lot into work. Sue and I had a little more time together and that was good. She was solid for me, as I was trying to figure things out.

It was time to start focusing on work. I was working at Cohesive. It was a great place to be with really good people. It wasn't like I hadn't been doing a good job at work while I was training, but it was time to put some of the energy I'd been devoting to swimming into work. I knew that my job wasn't my ultimate destination in life, and even that this part of my career was only a stepping-stone to something more important, but I didn't know what it was that was more important. I just knew it was time to start doing, rather than marking time.

What would I do next? Sue had made me promise no stupid stuff if we were going to have kids. I went back to the club a few times, but it felt empty without a reason to be going there, a goal. What was I going to do—just swim around a little? I renewed my membership at the club in 1997, but I hardly went.

I eventually let my membership lapse. I was putting a lot of energy into work. I pretty much stopped swimming. I still had my key for years after and I'd drop in and pay the day-use fee. But I didn't feel like a member. I found myself talking about the channel too often—like an old balding high school quarterback reliving the glory days.

I didn't have a swimming goal—how could you after swimming the English Channel? I didn't know that this feeling was common to English Channel swimmers, but I ended up talking to a few people who had done other crazy big things, and found people who got what I was going through. It didn't make it any easier, but it did help to know that I wasn't alone.

The empty feeling passed over time. I put more and more into work. I got fed up with my boss one day, took a call from a recruiter, and went to work at a big network company (3Com) when they made me a big offer. They had me travel a lot to Denver, but I had some serious problems with their ethics. It was a horrible place and I only lasted 6 months. Leaving was a very good decision.

I ended up going to work for a friend, someone my brother-in-law (Ed Hahm) had introduced me to. Alex Roosakos was (and still is) a great friend. When I was feeling pretty low at 3Com, empty and without any goals, I gave him a call and asked him if he would be interested in me working for him. At the time, I felt like I never should have left Cohesive. Jumping and going for more money, I had made a bad decision.

I'd done a little work for Alex on the side a few months before and it worked out well. I started a couple of weeks later. I worked there for a year before introducing him to the company I'd come to regret leaving. Cohesive was acquiring companies, and they bought Alex's company...I had my old email address back! He continued to run his "division" and started rising in the bigger company, folding other divisions into his, until he was running half of the consulting company. I likewise jumped two levels, riding his coat tails, but also because I was doing good work that was having a real impact on the company.

A few months later, the now bigger company (700+ people at that point) was bought, and we became a part of Exodus Communications. Exodus eventually became a billion-dollar company with 2,000 people before imploding in bankruptcy when the dot-com bubble burst.

Exodus had just gone public when they acquired us and I got a fair amount of stock (Alex took care of me). The stock immediately started rising. Sue and I now had a baby (Annika, born in 1999) and we took a trip to Australia. I made a fateful and lucky move (as it turned out, a very good one!). I'd been worried about the stock (a rational worry, as it turned out), so I sold everything that had vested before we left—about one third of my total options, and I just left it in cash. It ended up being one of the best moves I'd ever made. The stock (and everything tech) tanked a few weeks after we got back. If it weren't for that trip, I never would have sold any of it, and likely would have watched it fall until it was worthless.

We'd bought a house just before I swam the channel and the stock allowed us to pay off most of the debt, buy a couple of cars, and still have a very nice chunk of money left over. You can't always win, though. One might say I should have taken Larry's offer to join Google and be the 37th employee. The offer carried with it 25,000 shares of Google pre-IPO stock at a cost of $.001 per share. At least I'd proven my mom wrong—that was a worse mistake than quitting law school.

I looked at myself and decided it was time to figure out who I was, and who I wanted to become. Family started to take center stage. I also turned a corner with work. This was partly because I'd reached a certain technical level, but also because I'd turned a corner at a personal level, gained a level of maturity.

I'd lost most of the pounds I'd gained after the channel, but was slowly gaining weight again. We had another baby, Kylie, in 2001. We did some traveling. Life was good. I was in a good place. I was loving being a dad (still love it). I wasn't swimming, but the babies were great. We had a real family, a house, cars, good jobs. Everything was pretty damn good.

We were eating very well now. Sue got pregnant with Ethan who was born in 2003. Applied Materials fired her for that pregnancy. They bet that she wouldn't be the corporate employment attorney that sued her employer. They were right.

After Exodus, I'd taken a couple of short jobs that had paid well, and we'd decided to take a year off. We did some more traveling. I'd swim wherever we went, but I wasn't going terribly fast and most of the swims were in warm water.

I'd take the kids to donuts every Saturday. We'd get a dozen. The kids might eat 3…I'd eat the rest. Some habits die hard.

Between 1997 and 2012, I had been slowly gaining weight. I'd tried diets (1,000 calories a day, as an example), tried exercise, but whenever I lost the weight, I'd gain it back and more. I was averaging about 225 lbs. (102 kg.). This was a lot for someone who never hit 5'11" (1.8m). I peaked at 247 lbs. (112 kg.).

In 2010, I read an article about food. It had to do with calorie restriction. The article was poorly written, but I was realizing that eventually I would need to stop eating sugar. I didn't realize this would be months, not years, away. Nor did I realize that it would be not just quitting candy and sugar, but all fast-digesting carbs including potatoes, flour, grains, cereals, breads, buns; essentially everything but meat, fat, and vegetables. Then I read a couple of books by Michael Pollan. He's a great writer. Most processed food was off the table, too.

I was fat. I wasn't exercising. I was eating candy all day long. My blood pressure was high. My blood glucose numbers were not good. My good cholesterol was non-existent. To top it off, my cholesterol was high and my vitamin D was low, too.

What got me to realize I was sick were the gallstones. I had one the size of a racquetball and a few smaller ones too. I'd been feeling horrible for a while, downing antacids like candy (which meant a lot every day). One night when the pain was especially bad, I cried like a baby and Sue brought me to the hospital. After a lot of morphine to help with the pain, I had laparoscopic surgery early the next morning to remove them. The largest was the size of a racquet ball, about a dozen in total.

My recovery only took 2 or 3 days. I thought I would start feeling better and start to lose weight. Instead, the opposite happened. I started feeling more sick and gaining weight.

One other thing had happened a few times. I'd woken up on the car on the side of the freeway, in about the same spot, roughly 15 miles south of In-And-Out-Burger on Highway 580. The passenger window was cracked open, my seat was rolled back, the music was tuned to classical, and I didn't remember much of anything after eating the first few bites.

I figured it was time to try cutting sugar and starch. I didn't know what I was doing yet. All the doctors kept telling me was that I didn't have diabetes, and I already knew that.

I wanted to go at it 1000% (if you couldn't have guessed, this is my method for most things I do), so I started off by cutting all carbs, even veggies. It was hard for the first couple of weeks. Then I started losing about a pound a week and feeling better. I was more alert and awake and more a part of what was going on.

I kept my calories down, too, but after the first 2 weeks, it wasn't hard. I just didn't eat unless I was hungry, and I was mostly eating protein, which made me full. Later I added veggies, especially salad. The weight kept coming off—about a pound a week for about a year. At the end of a year, I was about 187 (84 kg.)—60 lbs. (27 kg.) lighter. When I started swimming again, I went up to 197 (89 kg.). I was 207 (94 kg.) for the Irish Sea attempt. But I was no longer fat and I was in control of my eating. I also felt healthy, much brighter, more alert, and I suspect, nicer, too.

How does diet affect a swimmer? In the short term, it doesn't really too much. Obviously, the diet I had for the English Channel (10,000 calories a day) was pretty much just a lot of calories with enough nutrients. At the same time, though, I now have a disorder that causes me to feel sick and then fall asleep if I eat sugar. It has many names (Insulin Resistance, Metabolic Syndrome, Syndrome X, Pre-Diabetes, Hyper/Hypo-Glycaemia), but not a lot is known about it definitively, except that it seems to be killing a lot of Americans. It was slowly killing me and I'm convinced I probably would have been dead by 50 had I continued eating sugar and starch.

Are all sugars and carbs outside of high-fiber vegetables bad for everyone? Probably not. Bad for me, yes. Young athletes can get away with a lot but as you age (probably even as early as 30 or before), you lose your ability to eat anything, even if you are burning tons of calories. Caloric equilibrium (calories in equals calories out) is important so you don't gain or lose weight inappropriately, but diet is also important.

Diet

If you're not happy with how you feel or your weight, try quitting all sugars and carbs including fruit and initially even cooked veggies, except leafy greens for 2 weeks. It takes about that long for your brain to break the dependence cycle that carbs cause (sugar addiction is like drugs). It will hurt a lot for the first week, and you'll be grumpy, even pissed, but by the end of two weeks. You will feel incredibly better, mentally more alert and healthier. Also, you will not feel hungry all the time. Your athletic performance will get better, too. From there, introduce veggies, and eventually some lower glycemic fruit. Never eat candy or starches again. It will be easier after the first two weeks, if you commit to it. Don't cheat.

We're just at the beginning of all this stuff with carbs. It used to be that fat was the bad guy. I truly believe that it is carbs that are poisoning us, but there is very little research that proves it (as a comparison, there is less scientific research proving carbs are bad than there was proving that fat was bad, although it now appears that fat and dietary cholesterol are actually good for you). This isn't a book on diet, but dietary sugar and starches are bad, not just for diabetics but for everyone.

The rules change for long training swims, but in terms of diet, fast digesting carbs are bad for your body and bad for your brain.

Bigger Picture

By this time, my career was going very well. I wasn't yet the person I wanted to be. I was succeeding in life by all outward appearances (money, nice house, nice cars, good job, wonderful family), but I wasn't settled. I didn't feel comfortable in my own skin. Things weren't where they needed to be.

I knew that there was something more out there. I knew I wanted to do more, but I didn't know what that was yet.

5 – The Split and Cobaltix

At the beginning of 2003, I started a company with a partner. We called it Iteon. I never did like that name, but my partner liked it, and I just let the name happen.

I didn't want to work for someone else. I was doing well financially, making a good salary, but I craved the chance to do it right—to run a company the way a company should be run, treat clients and employees really well. Working for yourself is not an easy way to quick riches, but we knew and planned for that. We both knew we would take a big pay cut. We grew the company for 10 years. I was the details guy, and he was the charismatic guy. We had 43 people including a company in Bosnia. We were reasonably profitable, as well. It took a lot of work, but by 2011 we had a pretty good company.

In 2011, something happened that changed all this.

In the second half of 2011, my business partner, who had become one of my closest friends, decided I wasn't good at running the company and that he should do it without me. Without me knowing, he had worked very hard to get me to quit or just leave and when I didn't he tried to turn people in the company against me. He tried to push me out of the company we'd founded together.

He'd worked very hard to get me to "sell" him my share for a very small amount of money ($3m over 5 years with lots of contingencies) and then when I said I wasn't interested, he told me that I could buy his half for $5m in cash (the company was probably only worth $7m at that time)—an amount of money he thought I would never be able to come up with. I hadn't realized we weren't friends anymore, and I worked every channel I had to come up with the $5m and even figured out a way to make the taxes advantageous for him. I still thought he was a friend and I wanted to help him do what he wanted. I wasn't quite sure how I'd run the company without him, but I knew I'd figure out a way.

We met at a restaurant for lunch so I could show him the deal.

He laughed at me.

He'd never intended to sell me his half at any price. I realized it had all just been a way to exhaust and distract me while he worked to demonstrate that I was a poor leader, and that I was so engrossed in my own things that I didn't care about anyone or the company.

I'd been trying to hold things together, hoping he would see that our partnership was worth saving and that our friendship was valuable. I was actually more thinking about our friendship than the asset that the company had become. I saw what was happening that day at lunch, but told no one except Sue. I'd been telling myself (and probably Sue) things like, "it'll all work out fine, I'm sure" which is what I believed.

I had been assuming the fault was with me. I'd talked to my dad and a couple of friends about being a better leader, but as it turned out, that wasn't the big problem. The big problem was that my partner had outgrown me and I was the problem for him. He wanted to run a company by himself, and I was still his partner. I was dead weight in his mind.

I didn't want to admit what was happening to anyone, but it finally became necessary on my 45th birthday, December 12, 2011. I had brought Annika to work with me that day (she was 12). I was heading home with her in the car at the end of the day when a call came in from my partner. As I'd trained Annika to do, she stayed silent while I handled the call on my car's Bluetooth speakerphone. He proceeded to berate me, telling me how much of a loser I was. He was swearing at me and told me how everyone in the company was against me, and how I needed to just give up.

In that moment, I had two thoughts. I thought about how so many people jumped to their deaths in 1929 rather than coming home to face their families. I had a small appreciation now for why. I was going to be ok, but I could really relate. The more important thought though, was, that I needed to help Annika understand what was happening and help her feel safe. I needed to be honest, candid, and transparent with her, the way my parents would have been with me.

It was time to figure out how to get through this. He was no longer my friend.

I explained everything to her on the car ride home and into the evening. Really, everything. Including how I was feeling, my fears, and my worries. I also told her what it wasn't. We were fine financially. We talked for hours after we got home, too, until she went to bed. I included Kylie in part of the conversation as well (she was 10), but Ethan (8) wasn't really interested. Annika wanted to know if we were going to have to sell the house and if we were going to have to move. I reassured her that we wouldn't have to move, and that we didn't need nearly as much as we had…that mom still had a very good job, no matter what happened with the company.

My old partner thought he was far better at negotiating than he was, though. He had borrowed money from the company, told people things that weren't true, violated our partnership agreement, and he thought he knew a lot more about how the company ran that he really did. He was not in a good position.

We ended up splitting the company. I gave him everything he wanted (I was extremely fair), but with the debt he owed, and what he wanted because he thought they were the most valuable parts of the company, he didn't come out very well. He chose the marquee clients (who were also the least profitable and least stable) and took the people he had hired (who were the most expensive and not the most talented). He ended up with all the risk and few of the real assets or best people. Also, we had bought a building in 2010. It hadn't appreciated much yet, but I knew it would. He didn't want the building. The building was all me, and he knew it, and he needed the cash. I paid him for his share. Five years later, the building was worth 4x what we'd bought it for.

For my part, I lost his leadership, his charisma, and a lot of my self-confidence. One of my best friends had made it very clear, and in no uncertain terms, that he thought I was worthless.

At the time, I saw this as the biggest failure of my life. It dwarfed everything to then, in terms of failure. It was someone I'd respected saying I brought no value to the table.

The split was hard on me—like cutting out half of my brain. In a lot of ways, it was like a divorce. I'd lost one of my best friends that began a very tough period for me.

Within a year, both the company and I started to evolve. Ironically, the company (renamed Cobaltix) was doing great. I was the details guy, and I chose the right things to focus on, but personally, it was tough for about 2 years.

Revenues, efficiency, and profits increased dramatically after he left with his half, but company morale was not strong. He'd always handled that. I needed to just move forward, but charisma wasn't something I had experience with, at least not in management context. I wasn't initially good at it at all.

I knew people liked me and they feared me a little, too. But I didn't know why morale was so low. It wasn't just that that it sank after the split, but it hadn't risen since, either. My morale and confidence had taken a pretty big hit, too. I was charting new territory.

Back in the Pool

In 2011, I started back into the pool. I had lost 60 lbs. (27 kg.) between my heaviest and my lightest, but now it was time to start getting back into shape. I could actually feel comfortable putting on a speedo (well, as comfortable as anyone ever could be in a speedo). I'd stopped eating carbs. I knew the pool would likely cause me to gain some of the weight back. It did. By 2012, I was back up to about 197 (89 kg.) but it seemed that I was adding back muscle. I was getting pretty fit (not just skinny). I felt good.

I went back to the Dolphin Club. I was feeling that going to the South End would be a traitorous act. Then I tried out the South End with Ranie Pearce. Ranie and I had talked about cold-water swimming at SODA, the pool I swam at in the East Bay. Ranie is an extremely accomplished cold-water ultra-marathon swimmer as well as an ice swimmer.

Ranie was responsible for getting me back in the Bay in the fall of 2013. She talked me into coming down to the South End Club and brought me down until I was addicted (I chose that word deliberately). Everything that the Dolphin Club had said about the other club was right. The clubhouse wasn't as nice, it was dirty, they drank a lot, their sauna wasn't as nice, and they didn't have any rules.

No rules...this was the club for me. I also figured out that there were no politics, and the negative attitude at the Dolphin Club just didn't exist at the South End.

I could swim farther because I wasn't just swimming in the cove (Dolphins aren't allowed to swim outside of the cove without board approval). I could still swim in the cove, but now the whole Bay was open to me. Also, the club had lots of people who wanted to pilot for swims. No need for board approval, and no negative attitudes. The South End wasn't stupid about things. You couldn't just take a boat out without being checked out, or swim to the Gate. But the caution was appropriate to the person and their attitude was "be careful, but your safety is up to you."

Within a few months (early 2014), I hooked up with a group called the Natadores Locos. Ranie was a member, and Kirk McKinney, Les Mangold, and John Sims (Capt. Mayhem) were the head clowns in the outfit. They did long swims. They rented the Hyperfish (Brent is the captain) and they arranged kayakers, about once a month. The delicious swims cost $125/swim, but they are worth every cent.

I was hooked. It took only a few more months for the water to reel me back in.

I hadn't fixed the morale problems at the company, but I was back in the water and that was improving my outlook on life. The company was doing very well (better than it ever had before with solid and consistent growth). But there was a sour air. Things weren't right. I knew the root cause was within me, but I didn't know how to fix it. I knew I could fix it, but I didn't know how yet.

The Birth of Innovation Labs

Sue and I had brought the kids to Europe in the summer of 2014 and one of the stops had been Copenhagen. While we were eating lunch one day, a very nice young girl, Andreea, waited on us. Now, this is not normal for Denmark. In that socialist society there are no tips. Also the Danish attitude of no one being better than anyone else (least of all the customer) creates an environment where service is poor. But Andreea was very nice to my kids. I struck up a conversation with her and it turned out she was studying technology, and she seemed smart. I gave her my card and told her to call me if she wanted to work in the US.

Two weeks later Andreea called. Her resume was quite good and she was very smart. I decided to fly to Copenhagen, interview her, and likely bring her to the US on a J1 Visa. A few months later, I went there. It turned out she was originally from Romania. In addition to Romanian, she also spoke Danish and English—both completely fluently. I think she had a couple more languages in there, too. She later started picking up Swedish, too. I'd later figure out that Andreea was even smarter than I'd thought. Not only could she pick up spoken languages, she could pick up programming languages even more easily. Hiring her was an easy decision. I was only thinking, "What will I do when her visa runs out in a year?"

While I was in Denmark, I did a little swimming in Copenhagen Harbor. The water was cold, but it was fun. The various things I was thinking about (Cobaltix, doing good, travel, swimming) seemed to be pointing me in a direction. I didn't know where, but I was deciding to let myself follow what seemed to be happening.

Andreea also introduced me to one of her teachers, Douglas Beaver. Douglas is a character. He's also a great judge of talent and a genuinely nice person. On that visit, I lectured twice, on entrepreneurship and cyber-security. In the coming two years, I would visit 4 more times and lecture about 20 times. He would introduce me to students and teachers, and many of them became either interns or fellows. Andreea was the first.

When she got to the US, I realized that not only was she an intern, she was also the start of something. I didn't fully know what it was at the time, but ideas were forming in my brain. My mind wasn't quite sure where this was going, but my brain seemed to be making good decisions. I continued to follow an instinctive path and was just saying yes. Even more, I was doing things, taking risks (highly calculated risks on the business side, but risk for me personally) and making plans that could end up failing. Fear, though, was not a part of the equation.

In the time that Andreea was in San Francisco, I'd realized that this whole J1 visa program was an incredible opportunity. I could bring the world a little closer together. I threw in a dash of "pay it forward" and had Andreea set up some of the structure for the "program." Andreea took my vision and some text, and applied her web and social media skills, and we started something. We started recruiting the next intern and also a fellow (no work requirement, just preparing someone to start a company). I let Andreea know what I was thinking. Andreea thought critically about everything, and provided me a great set of eyes. I was quite transparent with her during this whole process. She was getting a world class education in being a CEO (including seeing me failures). She also wanted to start a company. She would become the second fellow.

We came up with the name Cobaltix Innovation Labs for the program. When I went back to Denmark, I met with Douglas, who was now also bought in. He helped me recruit, too. Things were starting to roll forward, and Innovation Labs gained momentum. A lot like starting a company, you pretend that it exists for a little while, then some people believe you, then you realize that it exists, even if it is small, then you start growing it.

Andreea came in early 2014 and Innovation Labs was born later that year. The ideas came from me, but Andreea also had a lot to do with its inception. She made a lot happen. I still hadn't figured anything out yet, but things were happening and they seemed to be pointing in a good direction.

If I were writing this book honestly, every paragraph in it would have Sue in it. I've only mostly left her out because she is so infused in my brain that I feel like every time I say "I" she is actually already there.

I had exactly one person who I could talk to with completely candor after my partner left. I don't know how she listened to me through the split in that 3 months and as I was learning who I was now that I was alone leading the company. I'd tried initially to share leadership with the people at the top at Cobaltix, but that hadn't worked. We hadn't hired leaders, we'd hired engineers, maybe a couple of managers. Sue was my one confidant and although not a co-conspirator, she was there for me, every night for 3 months intensely, and the better part of two years, too.

Sue is an intellectual engine. She has the largest vocabulary of anyone I know and legitimately speaks three languages fluently, with two more that are passable thrown in for good measure. She is also an incredibly hard worker, a critical thinker, and an ambitious and successful person. Sue continued in law school when I quit, and ended up clerking in Federal Court. They also asked her to read for the Bar exam. She's smart. If I overhear people talking about "marrying up," I know they're talking about me.

We had a lot of luck in our careers. Every time one of us wanted to take a risk or needed to be very intense at work, the other was in a position to provide that home-side stability. This was true when we were changing jobs and taking care of the kids, too. It meant that we had a lot of leverage to take risks, and both of our careers have benefitted incredibly from never having to worry about paying the bills. We've always been there for each other.

We also supported (and still support) each other. Neither of us coddles the other (quite the opposite), but we're each other's best advocates and we talk through every challenging situation we encounter together. It doesn't mean we never argue (we both have quite strong personalities). We bring slightly different intellectual tools to the table and we brainstorm at night together, whether it is on kids, the house, our finances, our jobs, or anything else that comes up. She's amazing as a person and we are a powerful couple when it comes to raising our kids. I know she does more at home. I also know that she's in charge at home, too.

Sue never blinked when I said I wanted to fly to Copenhagen to talk to a young girl (who she barely remembered). I think she even knew before I did that I was getting more serious about swimming. Sometimes I wonder why she trusts me so much. I can always think of so many bad things I could be doing (I'm not—I'm good that way), but she always trusts me, no matter whether it is swimming, going places, or investing. She calls me on things when I'm using poor logic or about to make a bad decision. She questions me and makes me think at all junctures. Both her questioning and her confidence in me has had everything to do with who I am and what I'm doing. I'm incredibly lucky to have her.

Success

In retrospect, it makes a lot of sense that one of the darkest periods of my life, a time when I was doubting so much about who I thought I was, would usher in a time of clarity, a time when my purpose in life started to become clear. I didn't have the full picture yet, and I still had a lot to go through, but I was starting to see a clearer picture of what I was supposed to be doing with my life.

Steve Walker

Denmark

6 – Wild Sparks Extinguished

Around this time, I made friends with a few swimmers. One was
Amy Gubser. Amy is always positive, always happy. She was a
pretty quick swimmer at Michigan, but had mostly stopped
swimming to raise 2 kids, start and run a surf school in Pacifica,
and pursue a career as a pediatric nurse.

Amy had joined the South End just after I did. She seemed to know everyone, and I just assumed that she'd been there for years. We did a few Locos and Nutcracker swims together that Reptile had organized. We trained quite a bit. When I said I was doing Gibraltar (which was a test for me in many ways), she said she wanted to come, too, and I figured it would be cool to do it with someone I knew. I needed to know if I could go long without a lot of carbs and I needed to know if I was too old. I also needed to know if Sue was going to let me, I hadn't really talked to her about the whole swimming thing yet.

We got Amy's husband to pilot for us on a training swim from the Golden Gate Bridge as far as we could go North in the Bay, which ended up being to the Bel Marin Keys.

We swam about 21 miles in 8 hours at 55F (13C) from the Golden Gate Bridge past Tiburon, the Richmond-San Raphael Bridge, and up to around the Bel Marin Keys—about 18 honest miles (after subtracting the help we got from the tide). It went very well. From there, Amy and I started planning to swim Gibraltar, a swim that would probably take 4-7 hours and would be much warmer. Although shorter and warmer, Gibraltar is an iconic swim—between two continents.

Training is important. There are a few things important in marathon swimming and your training is one of those things that will determine whether or not you get across. The others are weather/conditions, the people on your boat, your mental game, and your cold-water acclimatization.

Swimming form is an important part of training. What you get from pool swimming is a consistent, efficient stroke. Open-water swimming is different from pool swimming (different form), but that doesn't change the need to be proficient and efficient in the water. It does take years to develop and it has to be kept up. It is easy to get lazy in open water and most open-water swimmers develop poor stroke technique because there is no coach.

That said, you don't get a lot better at open-water swimming by putting in all your hours in at the pool (although there are absolutely a small group of people who prove this assertion wrong every time they swim a channel). Pool swimming builds cardiovascular efficiency, lactic acid clearance, and also muscle mitochondria. The pool (for most people) will be the better tool to get faster but the pool doesn't help as much with building endurance nor does it help with acclimatization. The thing is that channel swimming isn't about getting faster. It is about going longer and staying stronger in cold water. Some of this is greatly aided by mitochondrial growth and cardio work. Some pool swimming early in the season might not be a bad idea, especially if there is stroke work, but regulating muscles and shunting in cold-water plays a very large part in being able to thermo-regulate and go for a long time at a consistent heart rate. I can't honestly or scientifically say that every swimmer should do lots of long swims in open water and very little pool swimming except in the early season, but that is what I do.

Swimming Goals

I've personally found that the first thing you want to understand is, what is the big goal? If it is swimming for health, you will take one path. If it is the Oceans7, there will be another path. Let's say your goal is the English Channel—a big goal, but also something that has been done by more than 1,000 people. Now you can start planning to get to your goal. After all, a goal without a plan is no more than a cloud, an amorphous mist, something ephemeral. A goal must have a plan.

Working backward, for any long swim, you want to have long swims to help your body become tuned to doing longer swims.

It is important to become proficient at swimming in the environment (and all that entails), to get better at thermo-regulation, and to have good feeling for the water. Feeling is far different in the cold, as you feel less in cold-water. Part of acclimatization is being able to feel your hands, arms, and body position when there is both noise ("stop this insanity, it is cold!") and reduced sensation.

Also, it takes weeks to become acclimatized to a given temperature, even if you are only dropping by a few degrees. The same is true in reverse. You can lose a lot of your acclimatization gains in just a few weeks. Long swims push your brain to train itself to withstand the cold, and make it to the end. Most ultra-marathon cold-water swimmers I know advocate doing 2/3 or 3/4 of the distance as the big training swim, ideally in the same types of conditions (temp mainly), 4-8 weeks before the main event. This timing also gives your body time to recover completely. The big training swim isn't a hard-and-fast rule, but rather a starting point. There are other ways to do it but getting in the distance is key. Without the mileage, success is not likely.

Getting to that big swim requires being in the cold a lot. It requires building up to the big training swim with shorter (but still long) swims. If you are swimming a 22-mile swim as your event, plan a 16-mile swim as your training swim at the same temp. This is often your qualifying swim, or if there isn't a qualifier, it can act as your way of making sure you are ready.

If the same temperature isn't possible, make the swim longer to account for warmer water, but also make sure you get in colder water, too. Then plan a bunch of swims that are 6-12 miles to prepare for the qualifier. To do the shorter swims, you'll need to swim most days in open water. Some people also do pool swimming (as doubles). Younger swimmers can probably handle more miles than older swimmers. Older swimmers need more sleep and recovery.

Many people advocate swimming the distance of the event each week (like marathon runners do). We have more in common with ultra-marathon than marathon runners, but the marathon advice seems to work well, as long as we do it in cold-water.

Know your body. Shoulder problems are not to be taken lightly. Have someone who can help you with your shoulders, not necessarily a doctor. A lot of times, this could be a masseuse or a physical therapist. Be wary of orthopedic surgeons. They always want to operate. They bring a hammer and every problem is a nail.

You shouldn't always quit swimming when you feel pain. Know what the pain is. Find out early. Find someone who gets athletes. Water is great for broken bones. Muscles and joints generally require rest, but rest the muscle, not your whole body. You can always kick. Nerves are harder. Figure out where the problem is coming from. Always think referred pain. Everything starts from the spine. Massage, stretching, TENS, chiro, and fixing your stroke are all good solutions when you have pains that are nerve related. Figuring out that something is nerve related is often hard. Enlist help: coaches, physical therapists, and massage therapists.

Don't be afraid of using Google. Google has limitations, but it is amazing how much information on our bodies is now available. Tendons and ligaments as well as other problems sometimes require different types of solutions, but often the root of the problem is in poor stroke technique. Again, find out what the problem is first. Get specific to figure out the root cause.

For training, swimming in especially rough water is very good. Also, swimming in smooth water is good, too. Rough water helps you know how to change your stroke, cadence, and body position when rough conditions exist. It can also be very rough on your neck and the nerves in your back. Smooth water will allow you to work on stroke and swim perfectly. It also allows you to vary your speed and get some speed and stroke work in.

In smooth water, do sets. Just like in the pool. Fartlek, 10x200s, 500 free for time, stroke work, even stroke drill (catch-up is a great one) if you can stay warm enough. It is hard to be disciplined, but if you can get all the benefits of the pool (sets especially), use open water to go longer and colder. It is always a good idea to get a good swimmer to watch your stroke every so often. It is easy to fall into bad habits. Get them to video you on your phone. It is invaluable.

All this is pretty easy. Simply set goals. Write workouts, sets, distances to cover each day/week.

Goals, In General

Goals should be SMART. This means Specific, Measurable, Achievable, Realistic, and Time Specific. I don't like achievable (it is the same as realistic). Also, you should never be so rigid in your thinking that you can't change your goals. What if you set the bar unrealistically high (or low)? What if work means that you have to scale back, but you still want to work toward the goal? The A for me stands for Adjustable. Smart people grow, learn, and adapt. Adjusting your goals is not a bad thing.

Once you have a goal in place, create a plan to achieve it. A goal without a plan is as ephemeral as a cloud of smoke. It is a wish, not a goal. When you attach a plan to the goal and start achieving against the plan, you have a very good shot of hitting your goal. If it is SMART, the plan is good, and you work hard, you will succeed.

I've used this method in both work (especially when managing people and projects) and in swimming to great success.

By 2014, not only was I thinking about my swimming and company goals, I was thinking about the goals for my kids. I was also thinking about the goals for Innovation Labs. More on this later.

At work, things were starting to come together, but I didn't have a plan yet. I'd put together a few goals for the company, but they were crap and I knew it. They were SMART, but they were also crap. I really didn't care about the goals I'd written a year before, in 2013. Morale was still not especially good.

I was starting to get there, though. Things seemed to be moving toward something...I just didn't yet know where.

Sleep

Cold-water and exercise requires more sleep. You will tend to sleep well, but you need enough sleep. At 48, I'm finding I need 7.5 to 8 hours of sleep a night. When I was in college, I was swimming and training 5-6 hours a day and was getting 5-6 hours of sleep. In law school, I got by for most of 10 months on 4-5 hours most nights, although the lack of sleep would have likely driven me crazy had I kept it up.

You can go on less sleep when you are young, but not as you get older. Also, even when you are young, giving your body time to recover (and getting enough sleep) will yield both far better performances (and better training), and also better quality of life. Sometimes you need to do an all-nighter, but just know you'll pay for it. Also, again, cold-water will make you tired. Get a lot of sleep—at least 7 to 8 hours a night, especially as you get older.

Stroke

First, stroke count is indicative of how a swimmer is doing. In cold-water, when there is a problem, one of the first indications is that stroke count drops. Most swimmers swim have a normal count of about 55-75 strokes/minute. This can fluctuate quite a bit, but most swimmers will settle into a consistent stroke rate within the first hour of their swim. During a "sprint" that can go up to 75-80/minute or higher (not as fast as pool sprinters who often go 85+). Also, cold water generally increases stroke count, as does a feed. A stroke count much above 75 usually can't be maintained for a long time.

More experienced ultra-marathon swimmers tend to have slightly lower stroke counts, but few are much under 55 and again, cold water causes an increase in stroke count. A drop of more than 5 strokes per minutes usually indicates a problem. That is very important for a crew to know. Stroke count tends to go down with experience because a longer and more efficient stroke is a big advantage in longer, endurance swims (especially stuff over 8 hours).

Although the front of the stroke is more powerful (speed for sprinting), it uses more energy and taxes more of the smaller muscles, especially the supporting muscles of your core under the traps. Conversely, the finish of your stroke is much more efficient, bringing in larger muscle groups (lats and more core) and it requires more roll, again using larger muscle groups. Also, a strong finish (although it causes a lower stroke count) pushes more water than a good catch. You can go farther per long stroke than you can with a sprinter's shorter stroke. A good catch is important for form, but less effort at the front and more at the back will produce a more efficient stroke. This doesn't mean don't have a good catch, but what it does mean is to focus more energy on the finish than the front of the stroke.

Also, with a longer stroke (longer finish), you will have a longer stroke recovery which will allow you to look more to the side for sighting. A longer stroke (finish) also gives you more flexibility to add in that front power when you need it and to vary your stroke if certain muscles get tired. In waves, you want to keep your pace consistent, and being able to vary your stroke (both inter-wave and over a longer swim) can be a great advantage.

A long stroke requires a lot of practice. Do catch-up drill (brush each hand with the other out in front at the end of every recovery). Try to train using catch-up. If you can get your speed to nearly the same level using catch-up, you will find that your "regular" stroke is a lot longer, and that you can go farther. Also, a finger-drag drill will force you to roll your shoulders, which is also a key to a longer stroke and better shoulder health.

I breathe mostly on my left. I can breathe bilaterally, but I'm about 10% slower when I breathe bilaterally. I am fully aware of the fact that breathing on one side over many miles puts uneven pressure on my spine and nerves and extra wear on the muscles on my left side. Sometimes (especially when it is rough), I really pay for it. I can switch to bilateral, but it would be better if I got good enough to breathe bilaterally all the time. Everyone has something to fix. I'd highly recommend breathing bilaterally. At least get reasonably good at it. You'll need it in a hard swim. This is advice I should take more seriously, myself.

If you are going to do pool swimming (for speed), there are two schools of thought:

1. Do a lot of sprinting in the pool and do your distance in cold-water; work speed in the pool.
2. Do longer pool sets. Use the pool to increase mileage.

I do the latter, but I better to do what you feel is right. Either way, you want to use a clock for every set. You want to be tired when you get done. You want to go fast and focus on speed over many repeats. You want to focus on the clock.

Many people don't swim much or at all in the pool when training for cold water events (I am one of them), but not everyone can swim year-round in open water. The advantages of only swimming in cold water are better acclimatization and longer swims with recovery also in cold water. It is also best to practice in the medium in which you swim (specificity), including taking feeds in open water, and thinking in terms of miles instead of yards.

If you are going to swim in the pool (sometimes you don't have a choice) and you are focusing on sprinting, do a lot of short distance sets like these (all sets assume a 25-yard pool, adjust intervals to correct speed and/or for a SCM or LC pool):

- 10x100 @ 1:15, or something that will give you less than 5 seconds rest (the rest of the intervals are based on a 1:15 base)
- 200s @ 2:45, until 3 at the exact same pace (to the second)
- 5x200s @ 3:00, set a target time for the 1000 and hit it
- 25-50-75-100-125-150-175-200, and back down @ :20 per 25, even distances are fast
- Same set, but with 10 seconds rest between each
- 6x [100, 125, 100] @ 1:30 for all
- 10x [100 free + 25 GOLF + 25 no breather] hold time for 100s, descend GOLF, 1 min rest after each 150

Swimming these types of sets, shoot for a minimum of 4,000-4,500 yards/meters each workout.

If you are focusing on longer sets in the pool (maybe you can't get to cold-water every day), try some like these:

- 4x400 @ 15 seconds rest, hold or descend pace
- 5x[2x200] @ 2:45, negative split each pair
- 4x1000 with 1 minute rest
- 6x500 @ 6:40, descend 1-3 and 4-6
- 1600-800-500-400-300-200-100-50-25 (and a 25 easy), hold the same pace for all, 15 sec rest
- 100-200-300-400-500-400-300-200-100 @ 1:15 base up, and 1:20 base down, even split all
- 5x [500 fr+100 ez-kick+50 w/2 breaths], 1min rest ea 650

If you are doing distance in the pool, try to get in a minimum of 5km per workout. If you're under 30 years old, go farther.

Wild Sparks

In late 2014, Douglas introduced me to two young women. They were best friends. One was quite smart and had some sales talent. The other seemed nice, not dumb. I was eager to create an opportunity. I wanted them to come to the US as fellows. The idea of the fellowship is that it is for young, talented entrepreneurs who are almost ready to start something. I'd brought Michael Cleverly over and he'd worked out well. He went to Haiti as part of his stay. He was my guinea pig, and I'd learned a lot about how to mentor incredibly talented people.

My instincts said that Marielle had talent. By herself, she was not the complete package that I look for (not strong on the technology side), but she knew how to sell. Andreea's brilliant, but she didn't yet know how to sell. Charlie (Marielle's sidekick) came along in the deal. My plan was to have the three of them form a company in Copenhagen.

I saw signs of trouble early, but I unwisely chose to ignore them. The two girls came to the US for a month (through Innovation Labs) and, within a week, they decided to bail. At the time, it was frustrating (to say the least). In retrospect, it was the best thing that could have happened. Wild Sparks (the name of the company we'd had such a hard time coming up with) was a dead on arrival. I cut the losses quickly and did what I could to help Andreea regain her confidence.

Andreea and I were starting a company, whether the girls were involved or not. Their exit delayed us a couple of months, but it steeled our resolve. Andreea didn't have the sales talent that Marielle had, but we decided that the learning curve would just be that much harder. Cobaltix could give her enough work to survive for a year at least (probably two), and give her some time to get her legs under her. We split the company 50/50 and gave her a salary from the work Cobaltix guaranteed. The hardest part, and I knew it would be, was that she was alone in Copenhagen. I was in San Francisco, and even talking every Friday would not make it any easier. I knew she was tough, though. She was.

That first year was really hard on Andreea. Starting a business is just like a big swim—you can't predict what will happen. You make a plan, then you execute to the plan until things change and the plan goes out the window. Not having anyone or even an office was difficult. If lack of business or poor sales don't kill a company in the first year, the isolation of being the only person running the company usually will.

We launched the new company, SA935 a few weeks behind schedule and few people even knew that there had been a change of plans. SA935 is the flight designation for the SAS flight from Copenhagen to San Francisco. It fit!

Taking risks was good. Even failure was good. Strength comes from failure.

Jacmel, Haiti

7 – My Worst Fear Realized

In 2014, the non-compete my former partner and I had agreed to expired. Right when it did, my old partner recruited a manager we were about to fire. What I didn't know was that they had been conspiring for months. I eventually found phone records. That manager brought our biggest client, 20% of our revenues, and 5 engineers with him. Ouch. Before it was done, we'd lost or fired 5 more—40% of the company at the time.

Having a mass exodus, a cascade of engineers leaving, especially one that affected clients, had been my worst fear—even before the split. Then it happened.

Funny thing, though, we survived and actually came out stronger. The blood-letting got rid of everyone who wasn't loyal (and a couple who just not engaged). They trickled out, so I was able to backfill the positions, our portfolio of clients became less risky, and we grew as a result. It was tough, both emotionally and from a business perspective, but sales were incredible that year, so we ended up far ahead of where we were the year before. Even profits were higher because many of the highest paid people had left (and my old partner was now paying them more, and making less from the big client—he was never good at the details).

Funny, too, but I'd also gotten an offer for the company that was very nearly "my number." I decided not to take it, but it was a huge boost to my confidence.

The exodus culminated while I was in Haiti (ironic that I was in a place known for violent coups) while I was negotiating the offer and trying to sort out what was happening. Haiti put a lot of things in perspective.

Haiti was about my daughter. She and I had talked about her doing something—both for her to grow and also to help set her college application apart. She'd asked if I could help her find something where she could help people by using her French, possibly incorporating in photography and travel. We met Jen and Guy (pronounced like the G in good, and the vowels in key—"Gee") in the Mission (through a friend of a friend). They run Zanmi Lakay, an organization that helps street kids in Haiti.

I don't ever just give money...it isn't my philosophy. I want to be involved, and I want to make sure the kids learn this, too. I'm glad to give money but if you're not on the ground you aren't really giving. We were on the ground, for sure.

We brought 20 laptops that we refurbished and set up a computer lab. Annika taught the kids in French, and they gave back to her by teaching her Haitian Creole. Power was inconsistent. Internet was nearly non-existent. Food was scarce, rice and beans was breakfast, lunch, and dinner, maybe with a little ketchup or sometimes tiny amount of chicken or vegetable to be shared by 100+ kids.

Water was not clean, but the kids were great. The kids we were working with were eager to learn, although they came with very little education. We had about 45 kids ranging in age from 12 to 22. About a third could read and write in Creole at a 7th grade level. A third were at a 4th grade level, and a third were at a 1st grade level. Some could speak just a little French and fewer a little English. We taught them Word and PowerPoint, although I'm not sure just how much stuck. We also taught them some basic business skills with similar success. They had a lot of fun, and while none of them can jump into an office job, they learned a lot.

Leading

It was while I was in Haiti that I decided it was time to lead—to not just try to make up for the hole my old partner had left (from a leadership perspective), and not just to recover from the turnover. I decided to take a step up, to take some real risks at a personal level, and become a leader. I figured out that it was time for me to lead, and not just by trying to figure out what was missing. It was time to lead by being me.

Getting the offer was the first piece of the puzzle for me. I realized that I was a leader. The company had grown and here was a nice offer on the table. I wouldn't ever need to work again if I chose to take it. I had led and there was evidence that with me as the steward, Cobaltix was demonstrably worth more than the company (both halves) had been before the split and that each person at the company was better off than they had been before.

I hadn't known what a leader was to that point. It had been first framed by my partner, then by his absence. I tried to find it in books and by talking to other people I considered leaders. I was slowly figuring it out. The definition of a leader was me.

I still had the last piece of this leadership puzzle to fix—morale.

I read a book on charisma (only found one that was any good, called, *The Charisma Myth*, by Olivia Cabane). The book basically said charisma is the product of power (the ability to do things for people) and being liked, which is accomplished by making every person know that you want to use that power to benefit that person specifically. I have always cared about people, but I was realizing that even though I did good things for people, I didn't have and wasn't projecting confidence. Who would want to follow someone who wasn't sure they were a good person to follow? If I didn't believe it, other people wouldn't either. Since the split, I'd been hiding. I feared that I wouldn't be liked and everyone would leave.

I realized that I wasn't lacking charisma, I was lacking confidence. Not everywhere, but just at work. That just wasn't me. It was time to be me again.

Fixing this problem meant growing. I realized that I couldn't ever (and wouldn't want to be) be my old partner (he had charisma in spades), but I needed to have confidence in myself as a leader. I also couldn't just be what I thought others needed. I had to be me, even if that meant some people might not like me, and some people might leave.

I had some confidence in my back pocket (the offer). I was someone people *should* get behind, and I knew it. I'd done well for every person in the company—raises, bonuses, benefits, learning and growing. In short, the company had become a much better place to work under my leadership.

As these ideas were bouncing around in my head, I realized I had confidence in spades when I was younger. I decided to channel energy from an earlier time. I thought of a time when I was coming off a low point. It didn't take me long to find. It was after I stopped swimming for Cal, back in 1987. Without swimming, I felt rudderless. I'd moved off-campus and pretty much isolated myself as I was ploughing through my sophomore year and a self-imposed heavy workload. I was watching myself and others from a third person perspective, not engaged in anything. I was cynical. I lacked the confidence that swimming had always brought me. Knowing my place, being an athlete. One day, I just decided it was time to end that period. I'd had a couple of small wins. I flirted with and met a few girls. It had forced me to smile and draw upon my inner confidence. I had to know that I wasn't just flirting to get a date, but I needed to *know* that I had something to offer the girls. By the end of 1987, I had regained that confidence and I knew it. It paid off in 1988 (a good year for me), and even more in 1990 (when I met Sue).

In 2014, I reminded myself how to flirt. You have to be confident to flirt. Remember, I'd been married 20 years at that point. This wasn't flirting with pretty girls as a teenager, although it was similar. It was showing that confidence, knowing you have something that other people want. It takes confidence, and also it builds upon itself.

In 2014, when I got back from Haiti, I turned down the offer. That took *huevos*. It was a risk, but it was also the right call.

Then I very quietly managed two people out and fired a third. One more left as a result, but that was a small price to pay for a team I could trust and grow. I also started to take charge. I wasn't leaving leadership to someone else. This didn't mean being "the big boss" or carrying a stick. In fact, it meant being especially conscious of other people, listening to people, and motivating them. It meant being the Steve that I knew I was. It meant knowing that I had something to offer these people; that I would be a better leader than anyone they might get at another company. I started smiling, being confident. It was like flirting.

Things really started clicking.

It took a few months, but morale improved. It wasn't all directly because of me, but everything emanated from me. I set the tone. I was working from a position of strength now, a position of real confidence, and others could see it in me. When people saw that confidence in me, they started seeing it in themselves and it caused a cascading effect—a positive one.

I learned from my failure. My failure was caused by weakness. It was not ***knowing*** I was a leader. It was not ***being*** a leader. It was not being ***confident*** that I had something to offer the people in the company. I don't know that I could have been the leader I needed to be before this point. I had to grow to become that person (and regain a bit of something I was before). I also had to own the failure before growing out of it. It was my time to lead and to be strong, to show that inner confidence that had been subsumed by the split.

Taking Risks

It was also time to start taking risks. To start innovating. To move confidently. To be willing to fail, even embracing failure as a part of the process.

I started asking a few hard questions. Why was I on earth? What kind of leader did I want to become? Who was I? Am I special or just another person making a living? What did I want to be remembered for? Did I have something worth teaching?

Giving back and paying it forward? Health?

What did I want from life? What was my definition of success? What did I want to be doing? Was this swimming thing just a hobby or something bigger? What was my definition of community? How was I making other people's lives better?

What did I want my tombstone to say?

As a dad, husband, and son, I think I do well. Any time I think about my family, it makes me feel good. It is my foundation and always will be. Nothing else can ever come first and I'd drop everything else to make sure it stays that way.

At this point, though, the kids are starting to gain a lot of independence and my parents are still healthy and active. With the kids, part of my job is to stay out of their way, to be supportive and there if they need me, but also to let them grow. With Sue, I want to spend as much time as I can with her. That is the one place I have to be careful. Swimming a lot of miles takes a lot of time.

I want to be a good example to my kids, and someone my wife and parents can be proud of. It was time to start growing.

100-Year Goal

In 2011, just after we bought the building but before the split, I had a mini-epiphany in the car driving to work one day. Even though it was more likely a small aneurysm, not a revealing insight, it led me to the delusions I am about to reveal to you (when I say, you, I mean my wife and my mom, likely the only two people who will read this book, if they get this far). I do hope this is not a small thing, that it will eventually be bigger than the company. If I succeed, I hope it will change the world. If I fail, I'll at least help a few good people.

So first, what was this idea I'd had in 2011? The idea was to do "something that would still be felt 100 years in the future." There were a few qualifications:

1. It had to be using ideas that I came up with. I couldn't just piggy back on someone else's cause or just give money, no matter how much I gave. It had to be something unique to me and be my feet on the ground.
2. I will need force multipliers. I can't do all this myself. I need to be a good leader to make this happen, and I will have to get others to believe in it.
3. This should be in motion by the time I'm 55. The interceding time is to be used as follows:
a. to become financially able to do what I want
b. to get myself together and be ready for this
c. to have a well thought-through plan that will lead to success. I want to be moving forward as I approach 55, not just starting to think about it.
4. It has to have a positive impact on the world.
5. It needs to be about expanding what people are capable of, by helping people understand how our brains work.
6. No one needs to know my name as long as I make it happen.

I thought a lot about what to do. Back in 2011, I had a goal, but not yet an idea. My idea is still not yet fully formed (I have a few years to complete the picture), but in the interceding 5 years, I came to realize that I do have two pretty unique things to give that could have an impact on the world and could move the world forward, if even a bit.

These two things are business and how we think. We are at a crossroads right now. Business schools are mostly teaching outdated and academic subjects that have very little to do with starting or running a business, and they aren't even doing a good job of teaching those things. There are "incubators" and "innovation centers" popping up all over, but these places are being run by administrators. The only real value they add is to put people of like ambition together. Some are becoming places to get venture capital. They seem to be void when it comes to actually starting or running a business, though. A person who is really meant to be an entrepreneur has no real avenues to be taught or mentored by people who have actually started and run businesses, true innovators.

Likewise, there are huge breakthroughs being made in a wide variety of subjects from economics to psychology, from neurophysiology to marketing, from communication to statistics, and in studies and articles that seem to be disconnected from any of these subjects. There are threads that tie them together, but it seems that no one has figured these threads out. These breakthroughs carry the keys to an almost super-human ability to peer into people's minds for those who can connect them together, and these threads can have huge ramifications in areas such as sales, relationships (at all levels and of all types), management, negotiations, influence, raising kids, achieving goals, dealing with challenges, and even in areas such as sports, marketing, and especially starting companies. I think of it as a super-power. The ability to see how things will likely turn out, and what people will likely do. It is not simple, nor it is really a super-power. Some people seem to come upon it naturally and others learn it over time. Understanding what the brain is capable of, how inherent limitations can be used to advantage and/or compensate for, and seeing these in both an individual context and in the bigger picture can have huge implications when taught well to the right person.

I can teach any smart, motivated person how these things work in a relatively short period of time (far less than it would take to get a college or even a graduate degree. It requires a customized program with different styles of teaching for each person, and a lot of hard work on the part of the person learning, but it generally takes about 3 months.

I don't have it all figured out yet, but I have figured out a few things that I don't want to be doing. I don't want to be a school—maybe a school of thought, but not a school. I've figured out that I don't want to teach this to younger kids (high school) or older students/people. These are things best absorbed by people in their early- to mid-twenties. Minds are open and can absorb a lot at this time and they're either ready for it or not. I can usually tell from a 30-minute conversation whether they are.

I've also figured out that I don't want to be an "incubator" and I don't want to be a VC. I'm not averse to investing in some of these people if they form companies, where it makes sense for them (and me), but this isn't meant to be a money making endeavor for me (although self-sustaining would be good). I come into this with a goal, and that goal is to give something back to the world, not to line my own pockets.

I've also figured out that I need to find those who haven't yet been corrupted by academia or a corporate (or even worse, a government) mentality. True entrepreneurs think differently.

They are open to ideas, open to risk, and open to failure—in short, still innovative. Schools and corporations have rules. Entrepreneurs break rules. Institutions beat innovation out of anyone who thinks differently. I don't need to get them already formed, but I do need to get them before they've been corrupted.

What I had to learn myself, really without help and through a lot of trial and error, took me years. Much of this can be taught, though, in a relatively short period of time—a lot less time than college. A part of it is teaching people to evaluate and take risks.

My goal is to teach people who will use it for good, and who will grow the ideas themselves over a period of years. I still need to figure out how this will positively affect the world, but I think I have the right first step. If those I mentor start companies, they'll create jobs. If they, in turn, use it to do good (pay it forward), it will have modest success. If they teach it to others the success will be far greater. The broad brushstrokes are there, but until I have a plan to execute against, it isn't rolling yet.

Innovation Labs has been my first step. It is working well. We've started 6 companies so far, two have failed (without any big ramifications, and we learned different lessons from each).

We are still early but at this stage, we're hitting our goals. The challenge will be to gain critical mass. Connecting each person to the others will be important. At a certain point, it will gain its own velocity and momentum. This is the goal. There is still a long way to go.

I don't know how this will turn out. It could be a a modest attempt to help a few people, or as a school of thought that changes the world. More likely it will be something in-between, hopefully toward the latter. Whatever it is, I'm having a lot of fun. It is a good thing. My goals are ridiculous, but if I hit any of them (100 years from now), it'll be pretty cool, even if I'm long since gone.

While I do admit that what I'm hoping to do may be a bit delusional, let's say I fail (as you've seen, I fail a lot). Even if I do, I will have helped many good people. It doesn't interfere with me making a living or supporting my family. It allows me to travel and my swimming seems to weave in nicely. And, I get to read a lot and think critically. Kind of ideal for me.

But, what if I succeed?

What if I could move the world forward at a more rapid pace? The mentoring and thinking could cause new companies to be created. It could change the economy. It could make life better for people. Others could pay it forward. This is a goal, that although somewhat lofty, is front and center in the fellowship program. I've already seen it happening on a small scale— fellows doing good for others. A cascade effect. It is possible. Who knows, it could happen!

I've found that I'm very good at choosing people to be a part of Innovation Labs and we have already helped them some to accomplish some amazing things that otherwise wouldn't have been possible.

I hope I do a lot of good. If I fail, I hope I merely do some good. Either way, though, it is a win.

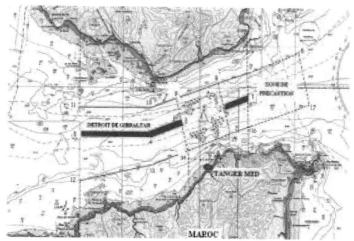
Strait of Gibraltar, Spain to Morocco

8 – Europe to Africa

In 2015, I swam Gibraltar then took a trip to Copenhagen where I also swam in water that was quite cold. I was 47.

Age

The effects of age on ultra-marathon cold-water swimming are interesting.

I lost my speed in my 20s. I lost my power sometime in my 30s (although I don't know exactly when—I was too fat). What has still remained is stamina and endurance, and a feel for the water.

As I write this, I am now 48. At 48, I cannot even touch the times I did in the pool in college. I went sub 4:40 in the 500y free (I was slow for Cal). On a good day, I might be able to do 5:40 now, which wouldn't even beat some of the JV girls in our neighborhood. Likewise, I can't lift a fraction of what I did in college, nor do I have that pure, lean strength I did even 15 years ago.

At 48, it takes me a long time to recover from longer swims. I need more sleep. I have to eat healthier if I don't want to feel like crap. It takes less to make my back and neck hurt. I'm less flexible. I do get it. I'm getting older. What is coming will probably not be any better. Perfect days are few and far between, and I can't just train tired for days on end. It doesn't work.

I also know that I'm lucky...my body still performs pretty reasonably when I treat it well.

Given all this, it might come as a surprise when I say that I'm a faster cold-water ultra-marathon swimmer now than I was 25 years ago. It isn't even close.

Let me repeat this: I'm slower than I was at the 500 free in a pool (by a lot), but I'm faster in a 10-mile (16km) swim in cold-water (by a lot).

At marathon distance in cold water (in swimming, 6.2 miles or 10km is the definition of a marathon), I can go a 21:30 mile pace or about 2:15 for the 10km. Granted this isn't all that fast compared to the fastest marathon swimmers who go under 19 minute miles for a 10km race finishing under 2 hours (although usually in warmer and flat water). But an odd thing happens over longer distances and in cold water. I only get a little slower.

Over longer distances, it seems to get harder and harder for younger kids to keep up with me, especially as the water starts to get colder. Most of the best swimmers I know in this discipline are over 35 and many are over 40. At 48, I'm getting toward the other side, but there are very good cold-water ultra-marathon swimmers who are older than me for sure. It is kind of like golf in that way.

Now, you might say, "Wait, your sport is a lot like a combination between hot dog eating and ice block sitting" (or sumo wrestling, maybe). Adam Kreek (Olympic rower) encapsulated the sport well: "If you put enough qualifiers (adjectives) ahead of any sport name, anyone can be a champion." To that end, I'm ranked #1 in the world in ultra-marathon, cold-water, swimming done by balding CEOs over 45 in the Bay Area (that I know about).

From talking to people, there is also an apex—a place where age goes from asset to liability. It seems to be at some point in a person's mid-50s to early-60s. This isn't to say that people in their 60s can't be amazing swimmers with great endurance and cold-water tolerance (even out-swimming kids in their 30s) but looking at times and distances, there is a point when the liabilities of age start to become greater than the advantages. Jeff Gunderson, a friend at the South End Club, is an excellent example of a person swimming incredibly into his 60s.

A side note about Jeff. About 5 years ago, he saved someone who was trying to commit suicide. As I'm writing this, Jeff was again at the same place. He was coming back to the opening between the end of the Muni Pier and the breakwater (Muni Pier and the breakwater protect Aquatic Park). Jeff saw a guy at the end of the pier on the phone. This guy didn't look quite right. Jeff watched him. The guy set his phone down and just jumped in. The fall wouldn't kill him; it wasn't more than 15 feet to the water. Also, the water was 54F (12C). Hypothermia would probably take at least a half hour to set in, possibly an hour or more to kill him. Hitting 54F water, though, could be scary and even painful for the uninitiated. Panic is the danger. In the cold water, a weak swimmer could panic and easily just start taking on water, go under, and not come back up. The guy wanted to kill himself, but Jeff wouldn't let him.

By the time Sofra (another quick ultra-marathon cold-water swimmer) and I arrived about 10 minutes after he jumped, Jeff had taken control of the guy, and talked him off the ledge figuratively. He didn't fight Jeff too much, and Jeff yelled up and instructed the people on the pier to call 911 and have the Park Service come out. The boat got there just before Sofra and I did. Jeff had just gotten the guy on the boat and was getting a little cold. Jeff is in his early 60s and doesn't have a ton of fat on him, but he's quite quick. I'm proud to say I know a true hero.

Back to age...something interesting I've noticed. Ultra-runners tend to be older, too. They aren't enduring the cold, and it seems as though the combination of the endurance and cold makes age an even greater advantage for more years, but it seems that endurance tends to increase with age. I'd really love to see something scientific. My anecdotes surely are not statistically valid, and the few studies I've seen have contributed little of value on this topic.

Why does age help so much in this sport? I'll make some guesses but again let's find a PhD student to research this!

First, on tolerance to the cold: Part of this is the ability to shunt, but that seems to be something that can be picked up in a matter of years, not decades. I'd like to hypothesize that a factor in cold water tolerance is being able to quiet the voices (noise from your peripheral nervous system). It might be like how when kids are little they hate coffee, but as they get older, their taste buds become desensitized. Maybe thermosensitive nerves get desensitized as well. I have better feeling when my hands are cold now than I did when I was in my 20s. I'm sure this has something to do with the amount of time I spend in the cold, but I'm sure it also has something to do with the fact that I can concentrate on feeling my hands and become more aware of the little useful feedback I'm getting. In short, I can block out the voices.

With the noise (pain), it is very hard to feel anything, but with practice the noise/pain can be quieted. Something like the ability to drink bitter coffee. Five-years-olds spit out coffee reflexively, but adults don't. Shunting is important, and takes some practice, but I think that this will cease to be as big an advantage as ultra-marathon and cold-water swimming gain popularity (as it seems is the case). Again, it seems to take years to master this, not decades. Blocking out the noise is harder.

Second, understanding bio-feedback around thermo-regulation and being able to make small changes that affect core temperature (more on this later).

Finally, there is mental toughness. Any woman that has gone through childbirth is going to be tougher than she was before the experience. Life tends to throw things at you that toughen you. As some people fail (and succeed), they gain toughness.

Tangentially, some people think that women might have a physiological advantage in this sport. They think that the slightly different distribution of fat gives women an advantage. Neither height nor being able to lift heavy weights lend a particular advantage in this sport. Efficiency and toughness are much better indicators of success.

At a broader level, there are more men competing in the sport at the elite level. But at the same time, more than half of all the world bests and most amazing swims are owned by women. One of the many reasons I like this sport is that the training and mental toughness are the biggest indicators of success and the usual physical advantages don't help. Only being skinny is a disadvantage.

A series of informal polls at the South End men's sauna (I see like 10 statistical issues with my poll, so just take it for what it is worth), suggests that many people get stronger as open-water swimmers until their late 50s or early 60s before they start to decline. Also, women have two advantages—fat distribution and a tendency to be better able to focus (sorry guys, women tend to be better at this than us).

Life has a tendency to make you tougher, and clearly those who can focus and have mental toughness have a huge advantage. I don't think it is a fluke that this sport has as many women at the top as men and that age is positive factor, decades past the years when strength and speed have started to wane.

Not everyone becomes tougher as they get older, but those who do get tougher, tend to be able to handle a lot of pain and are able to silence very powerful voices. Silencing the voices is something that often comes with age. This isn't to say that only older woman who've delivered their babies without drugs can swim channels, but I think what makes you tough will lend to success in cold-water ultra-marathon swimming. Anyone can do this sport but there are some things in life that would seem to convey an advantage, and those that lend to toughness would be first among them.

A lot seems to have to do with how often people swim in cold water, but regardless of distance or skill level, there is something to be said for the old saying, "Youth and skill will be defeated by age and treachery every time," at least to a point. It is probably fair to say that this sport tends to level the playing field. Those who got the *Most Improved* award as kids for trying hard are the ones who are likely to succeed in this sport.

Again, any PhD students out there looking for a longitudinal study of ultra-marathon cold-water swimmers? There have been very few to date and none statistically valid that I could see. I know I could scare up subjects for you.

Gibraltar

In late 2014, I reserved the window with the Gibraltar Channel Swimming Association. I'd be swimming in April 2015. It was quite easy to just modify it to be two people. Raphael runs the association. He is a very nice guy, but he uses lack of response to email to weed out those who are serious from those who are not.

After Amy and I did the 8-hour swim successfully, Greg, Amy and I made reservations. I tacked a few days onto my second recruiting trip to Copenhagen for Innovation Labs.

I did my 8-hour swim on a work-day so it wouldn't affect anything at home. There was no denying that I was spending less time at home. I was starting spend as much time as my friends who played golf. The trip to Gibraltar was ostensibly just a few extra days tacked onto a business trip. I'd asked Sue if she wanted to come, but that wasn't going to happen with her work schedule and the kids at home in school. Both the 8-hour swim with Amy and the trip to swim Gibraltar happened without too much consternation, but in my mind I was already starting to think about the Oceans7.

Kim Chambers is good friend (about a decade younger than I am) and an accomplished cold-water ultra-marathon swimmer. She has achieved all of the Oceans7. When I was getting ready for Gibraltar she was finishing the last few of the Ocean7 swims. I was watching. The 8-hour swim was a test, and Gibraltar would be a test for me. If I could do these, if feeds worked with my diet, if I wasn't too old, I wanted to do the Oceans7. It was as vague a goal as the English Channel had been 20 years before, but this time I had a lot more information. I was already a member of a community that had grown up quite a bit while I was gone, but there were still a lot of questions.

The conversation with Sue was the hardest. I wasn't hiding anything from her (I hadn't yet decided to I wanted to do the Oceans7, had I?). I had told her about Kim and the Oceans7.

I had kept my promise that I wouldn't do anything crazy until the kids were grown. I'd always assumed this meant out of high school, but how old was grown? Was this something I really wanted to do? Did I want to gain 10 lbs. (5 kg.)? Was I just pretending to still be young? Was this a mid-life crisis? Was I just showing off? Was this a young person's sport? Kim was 37 and single. I was older, married 20+ years, with three kids.

As I started to answer these questions, I knew Sue would support me no matter what. The funny part is that when we finally did talk about it, she wasn't too concerned about the swimming or risky parts, it was more the travel I'd do without her and the time away from home (both training and the actual swims). I felt the same way. I miss her when I travel and I like being around her and the kids.

I went to Gibraltar with Amy and Greg. We rented a car. Greg drove, which was very hard for me. I like being in control. I got us a very nice place about 15-20 minutes away from Tarifa. The area is beautiful. The day after we arrived, Agustin (my closest friend from high school who lives in Madrid) joined us. He was an incredible tour guide. We ate very well.

The weather was so-so. Not so horrible, but just not quite good enough to swim. The Gibraltar Straights can be treacherous, but also Raphael is quite conservative. He wants to make sure everyone can make it across.

On most big swims, you get a weather window. It is often about a week when the tides are favorable. "Neap" tides (when the moon is neither full nor new) are favorable because the tidal differences are less than during a "Spring" tide. This is good because the bigger the tidal difference, the harder the currents are to predict.

During a window, you hope for good weather. Usually light winds and calm seas are most important, sometimes fog can be a factor, too. You sign up a year or more in advance, and you try for the first spot in the window (pilots will usually take 2-3 people per window, hoping for a 3-day stretch of good weather, although weather is different in each channel. There is a protocol. You get your window, and if the weather isn't good when you move into the first position, you wait. If the window closes without a good weather day, you don't get to swim, and you go home. You still have to pay your deposit, but you only pay for the swim if you leave the dock.

If you have the first slot in your window, you will likely (but not always) get to swim. If the pilot says, "Do you want to go?" and you say no, you lose your spot, and the next person gets the opportunity. There is risk. On a so-so day, you might not make it. If you pass up a so-so day, it might only get worse and you don't get a chance.

In Gibraltar, the guy in the previous window, Cameron Bellamy had not had good weather during his window. He had been there 7 days and not gotten a chance. He was there with his mom. Raphael said he thought Cameron was about as fast as us.

We had the option of letting Cam swim with us. If Cameron was faster, he'd have to slow down. If we were faster, we'd have to slow down, or he'd have to get out (especially if we might not make it because of him—it was our window, not his). Some associations have a local rule that says you can't swim more than one person at a time, but there's no rule like that in Gibraltar. We didn't have to let him come with us (it was our slot, so also our choice), but if he was close to our speed, it was an easy decision.

We had dinner that night with Cameron, and found out that he is modest. He had done a bike ride. From the top of Scotland to the bottom of England. He'd also swum the English Channel (from his time and a description of the swim, it sounded like he was between me and Amy speed-wise, which was good). The English Channel thing came out about 2/3 of the way through dinner. Later that evening, I also found out that he'd cycled from Beijing to the bottom of India.

By the end of dinner, though, we found out something else about Cam. He did some rowing. I thought, "Great, what did he do, row across the Mediterranean?" I was quite wrong. He had rowed with a team (starting off with 7 people) from Perth to the Seychelles Islands, Australia to Africa, across the Indian Ocean. Fifty-seven days. Two hours on, two hours off. One of his team had to be med-evac'ed out when he burned his legs while cooking. Cam's stories were incredible, although it took us a while to pry them out of him.

After Gibraltar Cam and I talked business, and about 6 months later he ended up coming over and becoming a partner in a company I was starting. Turned out, he was more than a little smart, too. He also wanted to meet Kim. He not only wanted to talk to her about the Oceans7, he also wanted to go out with her. (I did eventually set them up. Timing was off, though...didn't work out although they're very good friends).

The next day, the weather looked good. Raphael said no, too much fog. We did a warmup swim with Cam. He was fine, right between us in terms of speed.

Another couple of delicious meals, then back to try to sleep.

The following day, we turned up. Cam had changed his tickets (as had his mom, who was supposed to fly back to South Africa, where Cam was raised). The swim was a go.

We couldn't have had better conditions. For the first half of the swim, the water was glass. The water was a perfect 66F (19C). I swam quite a bit of backstroke to keep down with Amy and Cam (who were, at that time, about the same speed). About 2:30 into the swim, it became a little less perfect, but still easy...no real waves, just a little current that was pushing us toward Africa diagonally.

We saw dolphins and pilot whales on the way over. It was such a relaxed swim. Ranie had told me to enjoy the swim and I did. At about 1km from Morocco, they told me I could open it up, so I did. I took off, finishing in 3:59. It was no record, but I had a great swim for sure. Cam and Amy were just a few minutes behind me. I'd like to say my time was fast because I'm fast, but I know better. I had a great swim, but really the swim was fast because of the conditions. Either way, though, it is always a little nicer when someone says, "What was your time?" and the time is fast.

Vinterbad Bryggen, Copenhagen
"Vi er iskolde" ("We are ice cold")

9 – A Scare in Copenhagen

Andreea turned out to be greater than I'd imagined. During late 2014 and early 2015, Cobaltix Innovation Labs, the international fellowship and internship program that we'd started, began to really take form. It evolved quite a bit based both on successes and failures, and was starting to become the first step toward the

100-year goal. Another piece to this was that I wanted to be fair to both the company and to the interns (not giving them too little or too much), but I decided the programs were not to be focused on profit. It didn't mean that they couldn't create profits for Cobaltix, but more that profits weren't the focus.

This second business trip to Copenhagen was the start of a period of incredible growth. I learned a lot about myself, especially that the goals I'd created for myself were not high enough. I needed to think bigger, especially around Innovation Labs.

Big goals, all at once. If I needed more time or to shift focus, I could hire people. As long as the business continued to grow and stay healthy, a lot of things were possible. It was time to see how many things I could do simultaneously.

Confluence. I didn't know it was coming, but it was. Things were starting to come together. I was seeing lots of successes (and lots of failures, too), but I hadn't put the whole equation together yet.

Right after Gibraltar, I'd gone back to Copenhagen. Hypothermia took on a whole new meaning for me on that trip.

Hypothermia, Fat, Brown Fat, and Shunting

Skinny won't cut it, but being obese is not good either.

Cold-water swimmers have a layer of sub-cutaneous fat on them. Skinny people just don't do well in cold-water. I gained 50 lbs. (23 kg.) for the English Channel. It was both too much and not healthy. I did fine, but probably in spite of my added weight, not because of it. Moderation is a hard thing for open-water swimmers, because, in the words of Bob Roper, "Anything worth doing is worth overdoing." Bob is famous at the South

End club. He still owns the record for the fastest crossing of the Golden Gate, which he did in 1969. I'd say most this is a mantra for most ultra-marathon swimmers.

Gaining 15 lbs. (7 kg.) over "wedding weight" is probably a good idea for cold-water swims. Although fat insulates, it is muscle that warms, and it is best if a lot of the extra weight is muscle. The better shape you are in, the easier it will be to warm up.

People (well people I know) are always talking about "brown fat." Bears have it, so do babies. In theory, it is more insulating and stores more energy than regular fat. It also has a metabolic engine (mitochondria). It seems that not all adults have brown fat, and the amount that they do ranges from 0-200g (0-8 oz.), most of which is concentrated around the heart and internal organs. Brown fat is also called brown adipose tissue (BAT), and can help keeping your core warmer. There is very little known (at present) about brown fat in cold-water swimmers.

Shunting is when your body slows down circulation to parts of your body. In cold water this is mostly the skin, first. Next comes the fingers and toes. Shunting protects your organs (core) and your brain from the cold by reducing where the blood circulates (not much to the skin, hands, and feet). It causes your blood pressure to rise (not as much room for the same volume of blood), but it is thought to be very healthy to swim in cold water, and shunting seems to have something to do with it. The science behind shunting is pretty well established, but the part about cold-water swimming being good for you is mostly anecdotal, but there does seem to be something to it.

The real danger in shunting is not when you get in (although a spike in blood pressure could cause a stroke or another problem if it is too sudden or you have a weakness in a blood vessel). It is the let down when you get out. As the blood starts to rush out to your now warming skin, two things happen. First the blood in your core gets colder. Even if you are warming up, your skin may still be 20-40F (10-20C) below your core, and that cold when that blood starts going back to your core, your core gets colder. Hypothermic people often pass out when they hit the shower, not right when they get out. Second, the same volume of blood is now circulating in more space causing blood pressure to drop. It is best to always warm up a hypothermic person slowly. Sitting down is a good idea, too.

In very cold water or very long swims, it actually takes not just being in good swimming shape, but being able to get cold, and get warm again. That sentence likely sounds immensely logical, but it is incredibly harder than it sounds, even for extremely well acclimated cold-water swimmers. Your body has already shunted blood to the core to stay warm, so getting warm really involves increasing heat production (and thereby also heart rate), but without working to exhaustion or even close to it. It has taken me years (maybe even decades) to be able to finely control core thermo-regulation. It is normally something that is controlled autonomously—not mentally.

This might be the biggest one from a physiological perspective. If you go too fast, you'll eventually slow down and your heart rate will eventually drop when you get tired, which will cause you to get cold, again, probably colder than you were. If you don't bring up your temperature fast enough, your core temperature will drop. Finding that balance (the right pace, in athletic terms) is something you can train. Making small adjustments, especially if your core does drop, is much harder in practice, and involves both shutting out noise so you can assess your real core temperature, and being able to micro-regulate. All this is often happening at a time when you don't have enough glucose getting to your brain. Pulling small levers to bring your heart rate up (often just by a few beats) provides slightly more oxygen to the muscles and allows them to work just a little harder to produce a little more heat.

Although a person's strength and power diminish over the years (and recovery time increases), experience has an incredibly large effect. Also, it isn't just a mental game or a certain skill.

Feel for the water certainly helps. In rough conditions or when your shoulders hurt, it isn't just a matter of having a perfect stroke. You need to have a variety of tools (stroke variations) to use, and you need to know how to use them.

Knowing what a perfect stroke looks and feels like has to be at the base. Water polo certainly helps, as you have to be especially adroit in the water (polo players swim well even with people beating on them). A lot of tough experiences in harsh conditions hours into a hard, cold swim over a period of time help reroute your neuronal pathways. It isn't just something you can learn, it has to be something that comes naturally at a neural level. Remember, your brain might not be functioning at the highest level during a long swim. It has to be automatic.

For people just getting in, an old trick is to say, "It is warm." Anyone can tell you, though, it doesn't work.

It is extremely difficult to hold two contradictory ideas in your head at the same time because your brain is smarter than you are. It will choose the true one. This has tons of implications.

What works better is telling a truth (a different truth), like, "It is warmer than it was last week" or "It will be warmer once I get my heart rate up." You will have trouble thinking about the cold if you are thinking about warmth, but you can't lie to yourself. Your brain is too smart for that. You need to discern different shades of gray, or different truths. I've heard a definition of a CEO is someone who can hold two opposing thoughts in their mind at the same time. This idea of shades of gray is important for so many reasons, not just in swimming, but in business and in life. Shades of gray are what other people miss in business. Shades of gray make better analysis. Understanding the fact that there is not just one "truth" is one of the markers of a thinker.

Back to the swimming. Imagine that every nerve in your body is telling you it is cold, this is crazy, to get out, that your shoulders hurt, that your doctor would say get out, and you're just asking yourself, "Why do I need to do this?"

On those early mornings, it is dark and normal people are still in bed. Even the people that love you don't understand why you do this. Your family asks why you do it. Your parents constantly ask you when you are going to grow up. Even the people you swim with are weird—not even 6am Masters swimming weird, but really full-blown weird.

This is just swimming in the Bay. Doing channels is a higher level of weird.

Swimming a big swim is 1000 times worse than just an hour in the Bay. You have some adrenaline for sure, but when you hit the water, it is still cold. Although mental games do help, they only last so long. Your brain will figure out if you mind is trying to trick it. You have to establish your cadence as quickly as possible—not too fast and not too slow. For shorter distances and some of the races, you can set a faster pace, as long as you can maintain it for the duration of the race. You can't overclock it too much, though—if you die (when the proverbial piano lands on your back) you are usually finished. If you're not careful, you'll not only not keep up the pace, but you'll even have to be pulled. If you get cold and slow down, core temperature can drop quickly.

It is very hard to recover from pushing too hard because the only way to recover is to go slower. If you go slower, you get cold. You rest, you get cold.

Long feedings have no place in most swims—even in relatively warm water. Warm water would be 62F (16C) and above—even 68F (20C) is 30F (17C) below our body temperature. When you come vertical to feed, your legs dip below the warmer water at the surface. That can sometimes mean a 2-4F (1-2C) drop. You don't want that for long. Ultra-marathon swimmers usually spend a total of 30 seconds communicating with other human beings every 30 minutes, when they most need someone to tell them they aren't crazy and to keep going.

It is possible to recover from a drop in core temperature. Only extremely experienced swimmers can do this (and you shouldn't try to do it, except very near a place you can get warm quickly with people who know what you are doing). It takes an incredible amount of acclimatization and a lot of experience, as well as great physical conditioning. I've never seen a young (under 35) swimmer do it. It means swimming through the beginning stages of hypothermia. It is also very dangerous. Inexperienced swimmers die from hypothermia. That's how the woman in 1988 died in the English Channel. She tried to push through a level of hypothermia that she wasn't conditioned for.

Hypothermia is kind-of like falling asleep at the wheel. You first feel cold. You naturally try to speed up. Then you get tired and slow down. Your brain starts to drift. If you are out of the water, you'll have trouble with balance and speaking. Your thinking becomes garbled and confused, your speech usually becomes slurred, as well. If you're in the water, you wander off course. Things seem bright, and it also seems dark. Then your eye lids start to get heavy. I don't know what happens next.

I've gotten to the eyelids heavy stage. It is one of the scariest things in the world to know you're only minutes from being dead and without much will to change your course. I've heard that people keep turning their arms for a few minutes without breathing before they just stop. Fortunately, I've never witnessed the last stage, but I know people who have.

The Scary Swim in Copenhagen

Ok, the eyelids closing experience. Let's put this into something real. I was in Copenhagen in 2015, shortly after swimming Gibraltar. Gibraltar was a glassy, wonderful swim—pretty warm for April, and for sure warmer than I'd been swimming in.

Copenhagen harbor, not so warm. It was 46 degrees (7.5C) when I got there. I swam about an hour on my first swim. The next day was colder, 45 (7C). I swam about 40 minutes, stopped for a few minutes to talk to some people in kayaks, then I started swimming back toward the saunas. People in Copenhagen swim during the summer, but they "dip" during the winter. About 1:15 minutes into the swim, I started feeling especially cold...not just cold, but I was feeling that my body was slowing down.

I'd tried to pick it up a few times. Each time, though, my body stopped responding to the push, going back to the slower pace a little quicker. I felt like I was swimming in molasses. My arms felt warm as they'd recover over the water, and my heart rate was dropping from around 110 to more like 90. Then around 80. Then probably 70. I had been alert through this point, but then I started to feel sleepy. It had been about 10 minutes, so I was now almost 1:25 into my swim. Thinking back, I suspect that my blood glucose level had dropped (I hadn't eaten any breakfast). My eyelids started getting heavy. The light of the morning (overcast) was too bright. My eyes started closing. They'd be closed for about a second, then I'd open them. Closed again, a little longer, then open. In quite a daze, I realized that I was in a very bad place and that if I closed my eyes again I might just slip under the water and never come up.

I stopped and went vertical. I wasn't really moving much, and my core temperature was starting to drop quickly. I saw a ladder (I'd seen them before—always have an escape route) to get out of the harbor and back up on the promenade, which was about 12 feet above the water. I climbed the ladder. It was rusted. There was no one around that I could see (my vision wasn't too sharp at this point). I realized I'd come up in a fenced-off construction zone. The chain link fence surrounding it went out over the water. I started to try to climb around it, but fell back in. It was cold, but no colder than I was and at least at this point I was awake. Slapping the water (about 12' down) hurt a little, but I pretty much know how to fall into water without getting hurt.

I swam back to the ladder. The rusty ladder hurt my feet this time. Probably a good sign. I climbed up, then around the fence, successfully this time. Then I started walking nonchalantly back to the sauna. The air was making me cold, but it wasn't windy and I was warmer than I had been in the water. The air was probably about 40F (4.5C). I should have been colder, but I think adrenaline was kicking in...my heart rate was easily over 100 now. I started to jog. I couldn't feel my feet, but I was somehow landing my feet without scraping my toes on the cobblestones. There were people now. I'd stopped swimming about a quarter mile (400m) short, so I was only about a 5-minute walk/jog from saunas. I could see the people, but I couldn't focus on their faces. I was still too cold to see clearly. They were probably looking sideways at the bright red guy in the speedo running barefoot, at least that's what I was assuming, but I knew it didn't matter. I didn't want to be in an ambulance. I was telling myself, "Just keep going, pretend like everything is normal...need to be in the sauna."

I got back to the sauna, but I had to knock to get in (even though I was a member, I hadn't gotten my wrist bracelet yet to open the door). A couple of young women let me in. Even hypothermic, I still noticed that they had nice figures and that they were wearing bikinis. I was probably staring, although not intentionally. I got in, and after a few minutes, I quite articulately said, "Could you watch me, I'm a little cold." They probably were wondering if I was some weird inappropriate old guy who wasn't even a member of the club. I've acquired a skill—being able to talk while cold, and I don't usually shiver (I wasn't). I probably wasn't exhibiting any of the obvious signs of hypothermia. I'd imagined my words probably sounded completely insincere. They were probably thinking I was a complete nob with way too much confidence for the water they were dipping in.

If they were thinking it, they were right about the way too much confidence part, but they didn't know I'd been swimming almost 4 miles (6km) until I'd warmed up a little and started talking to them. I was in the sauna for almost 30 minutes before my body temperature was back approaching a reasonable level.

This was as cold as I've ever been. I hope to never go to that point ever again. It is a scary place and I was the only one who knew I was in such a bad place.

I was back in Copenhagen a few months later for Innovations Labs to do more recruiting and awarding internships and fellowships.

Technically, I'm not supposed to be swimming in Copenhagen harbor—it is a $50 fine, but no one has ever said anything. The people who use the sauna swim in a saltwater pool—not the harbor itself.

I was back in Copenhagen a few months later for Innovation Labs to do more recruiting and to award more internships and fellowships. I had another interesting experience. While was in the sauna a bunch of cops, a firetruck, and an ambulance showed up outside. I was worried that my days of swimming there were over. It turned out they weren't interested in me. There was a man who'd fallen in and died of hypothermia. He was older (70+) and had probably fallen in the night before (he was dressed). He might have even had a heart attack before falling in for all I know, but odds were that the cold actually killed him. I got out a few feet from where he had come to rest in the water, but I hadn't see him. He was probably resting just under the water, and I would have been a bit cold. I was feeling lucky all that day (and for days after)—not because I'd avoided a fine, but because I was alive. There were two of us in the harbor that morning, and I came out alive.

Ireland

10 – Irish Breakfast Is the Best

After Gibraltar and my very cold Copenhagen experience in mid-2015, I decided I was going to do all of the Oceans7. I asked Sue and as is so often the case, I was more worried about what I thought she might say than what she actually said. Her reaction was supportive, although a bit tentative about the time

I'd spend training and traveling. She even said she wanted to come to Ireland with the kids for the North Channel.

Game on!

I started training hard, and did a lot of hard, long training swims.

I earned a title at the club during this time: Rogue Swimmer. There are no rules at the South End, but there are still a few people who think there should be at least some rules. I'd swum out to the Golden Gate (more than a few times) and someone had seen me on one of these swims. Both Tom (Reptile) and Bill Wygant called me. They didn't ask me to stop doing "out of bounds" swims, but more just told me to not get caught because it made their jobs tougher. Reptile offered to help me find people to kayak, and shortly thereafter started setting up "Nutcracker Swims" so I wouldn't be rogue. Likewise, Bill was incredibly supportive. This was a night and day difference from my experience at the Dolphin Club.

I used the opportunity to drum up some help with a swim from the San Mateo Bridge. I was shooting for a nine-hour swim, with higher goals of getting to the club or maybe even the Golden Gate. We had a fair amount of chop and headwind that mostly negated the tide assist we were expecting, and only got to the club (20 honest miles) in 9 hours. Cam swam part of it with me, and Ryan Dalton swam most of the way. Joe Butler was the pilot—9 hours in a boat is a long time. I owe Joe something special. I still need to pay him back.

I don't consider the swim a failure (even though I was really hoping to get to the Golden Gate). We got as far as we could, given the conditions. I could have gone for more time, but the tide had turned and I was only going to be washed back. I did need to learn from this, though. My right shoulder hurt, and the swim had taken a lot out of me.

After the San Mateo swim, I'd gotten on a plane to Ireland and swam in lots of places around the island. It was the most incredible trip.

I started off by driving down to meet a guy named Donal. He writes a blog under the moniker of "Lone Swimmer." The name doesn't represent him well. He's a very social guy. If you like open-water swimming, you should read everything he's written; he's a great writer. Anyway, he brought me to a short stretch of coastline near Waterford. The water was cold, but not too bad— maybe 48F (9C). We swam about a mile, then into a pretty cool cave. I got pretty scraped up coming out. Then we went back. One of the best hour swims I've ever had. We went to a pub and had a bit of dinner. Donal said he was interested in being crew for me in the North Channel if the timing worked out.

Next, I went to Cork. I was hoping to swim at Sandy Cove with Ned Denison. I hadn't reached out to Ned, but I found it anyway, mostly just by asking people for directions. I met a very nice and pretty woman who knew Ned. Ned, by the way, is the unofficial mayor of Sandy Cove Swimmers and runs a swim camp there for English Channel aspirants. I found it, and just got in. I was swimming by myself. It was a beautiful day—sunny. In the middle of the cove is an island. The island is really nice...probably about a mile (1.6km) around. The water was warmer, probably 49 (9.5C). I met some nice people when I got out. The day was just turning out perfectly.

I drove to a technical university in Tralee. It turned out to be a bust—it was more technical like in terms of which kind of fertilizer and seeds to use, and how to fix farm equipment. But the drive and the town were pretty. After that, drove to Galway. Gary had let his mom know I was coming, but I only ended up there for an evening. I swam about 2.5 miles (4km) in Galway—just straight out to a buoy and back. The water was ok, a little colder again, probably 48 (9C).

After my swim, I had breakfast. By the way, Irish breakfast is the best thing ever invented. I took off driving after breakfast up to Ballyshannon (near Donegal). Bobby had set me up to stay with his sister Sarah. I got there early, and found a nice place near the river to take a nap in the car. My business trip to Ireland was not exceeding my expectations. I was hoping to meet candidates for the internship and fellowship programs, but I wasn't any closer (at least I wasn't thinking I was).

I called Sarah and we met late in the afternoon. We went to her house, then left immediately to swim. The water was colder (probably 47F/8.5C). We stayed in about 45 minutes. Sarah wasn't as fast, but she could sure handle the cold. We were each testing each other out. Swimming with someone based only on reputation is a bit hard. You don't take someone's life into your hands lightly, and you always want to see people swim, first hand, and see how they are when they get out. Needless to say, I passed her tests and she was quite capable as well.

Sarah had just gotten back from the European Lifesaving Championships. It is kind of like Masters Swim Meets in the US. She had gotten 2nd in her age group (I think 50+). She's no slouch. We also swam with another woman, Anne.

The next morning, we swam with a younger guy (I kept up with him pretty easily) and another swimmer (Brian) more Sarah's and my age. We went about an hour and a quarter. Both swims were great. By this time, I was getting used to swimming in the upper-40s (7-9C) swims. They were pretty shocked that I didn't need a towel and wasn't shivering. I was cold, but my body temperature hadn't dropped much. These were two really great swims in two days. I didn't want to overstay my welcome, but

Sarah's family made me feel completely at home. I was sad to leave, but promised to come back on my next visit.

From Ballyshannon, I drove through a bit of the countryside, seeing great rainbows and some incredible landscapes that I knew had been painted just for me.

I drove into Belfast, then through to Helen's Bay. I swam for the second time that day there (the temp around 46F/8C). I got a warm milk and borrowed the phone at the coffee shop to call Quinton. I met him about 30 minutes later. We had a great talk. He could assess my abilities without seeing me swim (or as much as he needed to). I was likewise sure that he's as good as people had told me. He is older with obvious wisdom and is able to read a person quickly (like Mike Oram, the English Channel pilot) but much nicer. He does not mince words either. We went to take a look at his boat. He also told me, no head on the boat. Likely no girls would want to go. That made it easier. I wouldn't have minded someone on the boat, but I wasn't excited about having Sue or the kids. This swim was going to push me to the very edge, and I didn't think that having anyone on the boat who really loved me would be a good idea.

After my meeting with Quinton, I went to my B&B (which was very nice). The next morning, I had a great breakfast. I'd done 6 swims in 5 days, so I decided to skip a day before Copenhagen. Then I took off and drove down to Dublin for my flight.

On that drive, I had a couple of hours to think. The radio was on, but not bothering me. I thought of a good word—confluence. The word had been chasing me for a while. It represented a lot of the things that were happening in my life. My 100-year goal, travel, lectures, swimming, the fellowships and internships, the good things Annika was doing in Haiti, Trinity (I'd bought half of our old family property in Trinity county, in Northern California), Cobaltix—everything seemed to be connecting back to each other. Things were starting to come together—not perfectly, but I started to see some things clearly on that drive that had been quite fuzzy before.

The next week in Copenhagen was good. I got 3 swims in. The water was 45F (7C) the first day, and 44F (6.5C) for the second and third days. I swam 45 mins the first day, an hour on the second, and a quick 15 minutes on the third day.

Confluence

Innovation Labs was in full swing. I recruited another great intern (Andor) and gave two successful lectures. On the way back home, I stopped in Dublin for a night, getting a short swim in and one more Irish breakfast. Things were coming together. Business was great, too.

I recruited two other great people in Copenhagen. Laura, a bright star; different from the others. She'd later turn out to be one of the best recruits I'd find. I'd learn a lot in teaching her, especially that one size does not fit all in terms of how to choose people and how to mentor. She caused me to think about finding people differently.

Martyna was another great find. Still haven't figured out the formula with her, but she keeps exceeding my expectations. I think that is just how she is going to work.

I had learned from my failures and was now starting to enjoy some success. I was keeping a lot of balls in the air. Ten different things were moving forward. Things were happening in Ireland, too.

I was ready for whatever was coming next.

Santa Catalina Strait

11 – Catalina

About 5 weeks after San Mateo and a week after the
Ireland/Denmark trip, on Thursday, November 7, 2015, I got in
the car with Cam and Amy, and drove down to LA. I was
supposed to sleep in the car on the drive down, but I couldn't.

Once we found the San Pedro pier, we got dinner (cheese omelet for me) at around 6pm and met Reptile and Dan Simoneli, who is a great kayaker/swimmer from San Diego that Ranie Pearce had helped me arrange.

We then met the pilot who was going to take me from Catalina Island back to the California Coast. The pilot had a pretty big boat (much bigger than I was expecting) and a crew—a second pilot, a deck hand, and a cook. It seemed like overkill, but I'd already paid for it, and it this was clearly the way it was done.

I hadn't taken this swim as seriously as I should have. It is a big swim, and I didn't rest for it properly. My right shoulder was still sore from the San Mateo Bridge swim. I was still jet-lagged (only made worse by an 11pm start). I'd been swimming very short swims in Ireland and Denmark in cold water. Catalina was warm (66-70F, 19-21C). I had not only pain but also weakness in my right deltoid (upper arm, near the shoulder). It wasn't "shoulder pain" that every swimmer worries about, but it was hard to swim with. I'd basically rested for 3 weeks, by not swimming much. The swims that I'd done were all in very cold water. Hardly an ideal taper.

The fact that the swim was so close geographically had lulled me into mentally discounting how tough it was going to be. I'd thought,

> *Catalina isn't usually as hard as the English Channel. It is always easier than the Irish Sea—my next big goal. I'll probably go around 9 hours. I just did that 4 weeks ago with Ryan and Cam.*

I was supposed to sleep on the boat ride out, but I couldn't. We got to Catalina an hour early and we decided to just jump at 11pm instead of midnight.

I jumped in the water. It was luminescent—every stroke would leave a blue streak...really blue. There was a seal when I jumped in, and I could see fish and the seal through my goggles under water. The water was blue and beautifully clear.

I had a couple of bars in the last hour and a half before the start, and drank a little water. Feeds didn't need to be warm. I had a plan that comprised a protein drink and bars every 30 minutes skipping the first 2 feeds.

The first 15-20 minutes were smooth. I was going fast and on pace for the fast swim I was expecting. After we cleared the islands, though, the water started getting a little swirly. There weren't big waves (maybe 1-2 feet), but it quickly became "washing machine" conditions. I'd felt a lot of turbulence when I was on the boat on the way out, but I'd just assumed it was the boat. It wasn't the boat.

It really didn't get any better, but at first I was in good shape. I'd thought,

> *I'll just swim until the sloshing calms down. Catalina isn't going to defeat me in the first hour.*

I took my first feed at 1 hour, despite my plan. I was restless and wanted to stop to talk. They fed me. I probably shouldn't have taken it, but I did—it tasted good. It always does. I stopped again at an hour and a half in (now 12:30am, back on plan) and fed again. The eggs from dinner at 7pm weren't feeling so great. Not bad, but I just didn't have any energy. The bars weren't making it better either.

I was doing okay at this point, but things just didn't feel right. The whirling conditions hadn't gotten any better either.

At the 2-hour feeding, my stomach was not feeling so great. I just took liquid (25g protein, 4g carbs). I quickly realized that wasn't good. Within about 20 minutes, I'd gone from not-quite-right to feeling really lousy. My stroke count was increasing (guessing from 60 to 67) but I wasn't pulling any water. Not only were my arms not catching water or hitting what felt like concrete waves, but I just had no pull. My neck was also starting to really hurt from being knocked around by the waves. The waves still weren't big, but they were unpredictable with white caps, each one seeming to come from a different direction. My stomach was now in knots. It felt like a brick was sitting in there, rough corners and all.

I stopped at 2:20 (1:20am), and start to take a feed, but it got swamped. It tasted like salt water, and the one sip I took pushed me over the edge. I couldn't keep swimming.

I did a little sculling (like breast stroke, but doesn't propel you forward much). My brain was not working. My blood sugar was dangerously low—probably in the 50s or low 60s. If anyone was talking to me, it wasn't registering. I was just trying to concentrate on continuing, but I couldn't swim freestyle. It was better sculling, but I was starting to get cold (me, cold in 70F/21C water?).

I was in a bad place. I just kept sculling, not really kicking. The crew probably knew I was in trouble, but if they did they didn't say anything. The waves were washing into my head and my neck was hurting. I was swallowing a lot of water, about a gulp every minute or two. I'm not sure if I had my goggles on or off during this time. It was still dark (not yet 2am and overcast), and the lights of the boat were kind of blinding.

After about 20 minutes, I added a dolphin kick, weak at first, but I started moving, even if only a little. About 10 minutes later, I was starting to feel a little better and turned the sculling into breaststroke pulls. I was starting to wake up a little. At some point, I think someone offered me feed. I said no. I think the whole time I was communicating ok, but I don't think I was saying much. I don't remember much. At around 2:20am (3:00 into the swim), I took a little water (plain), then I started swimming freestyle again. I was pretty cold at this point, but at least I was now getting a little sugar to my brain and muscles.

About 30 minutes later (next scheduled feed time), Amy got me some scrambled eggs—just a half a paper cup full. It tasted pretty good—I was hungry at that point. I was starting to swim at a more regular cadence (60 strokes per minute), but was still getting pummeled by the washing machine waves. I remembered that I was going to be positive the whole way— even if I needed to be pulled. I told Dan a joke:

> *What do you get when you cross a brown chicken and a brown cow?* (Answer, with a 70s soul vibe) *Brown-chicka-brown-cow.*

During this time, I remember "seeing" a pier on might right (the side I didn't breathe to, so I wasn't even looking that way). If I looked to my right, it wasn't there, but it was there in my head.

Around 2:30am (I'd lost track) Dan switched out, and Reptile (Tom Linthicum) started kayaking. Tom is experienced. He was in for a few hours. I think around 5:30am, he switched out. The only thing was he flipped his kayak as he was trying to get close to the boat. He was a yard sale—everything all over the place. He lost a lot of stuff, including half of my feeds and bottles. It wasn't him, the water was turbulent. That should give an idea of just how hard it was to swim in, too.

From this point until about 6am (7 hours in), I swam, taking regular feeds (bars every other) but just water for my drink. I noticed it getting a little lighter and then saw the sun coming up to the south a little before 7am. By 7:30am, the waves had settled down a bit. There were still 1-2 foot (.5m) waves, but the washing machine had eased up. I was now 7.5 hours in and I knew I was nowhere near finishing. It seemed like I was going to be around 11.5-13 hours. I was getting pretty regular updates on distance and doing a lot of math. Likewise, I was also counting strokes. I was figuring that at 60 strokes per minute, 30 minutes was 1,800 strokes. I couldn't count that high, but I could do 300 strokes (5 minutes) 6 times. I don't think I ever strung together 30-minutes'-worth, but at least it helped me pass the time.

I was making consistent progress now, about 2mph (3.2km/hour) from what I could tell. They were giving me the measurements in nautical miles, so I had to do math to convert. The sunlight felt good. Even though the water was 66-70F (about 20C), I had been cold when I was having trouble and I never felt all that warm, but the sunlight did feel good.

I don't remember much from the next few hours. I just kept swimming.

Toward the end, Dan was back in kayaking and I could see where we were going to land pretty clearly. I was moving at about 2 mph (3.2km/hour) pace, but the darkness hours had hurt me time-wise. I was hoping to be under 10 hours (even toying with 9 hours, but thinking 9.5 hours). Here I was looking at around 12 hours. I wasn't feeling really positive, but I'd finish.

I just kept swimming.

As I got within about an hour, I asked Dan whether I could break 12 hours. It looked like we were about an hour out. He said maybe. I don't think he really knew, but I decided it was time to swim a little faster. I picked up the pace quite a bit. The waves and wind were starting to kick in a bit, but I swam about an hour at a much, much faster pace. My stomach was okay now and I just decided it was time.

I didn't make 12 hours (missed by 14 minutes), but I moved that last hour or so. I probably wasn't doing any record times with the wind coming across me. I eased off once I was past 12 hours, but not too much. I stopped feeding that last stretch. When I got to the beach, I ran up and grabbed a rock. I was in pretty good shape, despite the early part of the swim.

I'd honestly expected to do the swim in around 9 hours or maybe less. I'd been swimming fast, but I didn't rest well, my right arm wasn't working the way it was supposed to, my feeds were a disaster—almost ending my swim. The conditions were washing-machine. I'd made it, but in my mind this was a disaster of a swim. In my mind, I'd failed—nothing went as planned and I had a terrible swim. I had to concentrate on the one salient fact—I'd finished.

The boat ride back to the dock took about an hour. I got some bacon. I was in pretty good shape considering. We got some food on the way back to the hotel and then I slept for a couple of hours before the IMSHOF (International Marathon Swimming Hall of Fame) dinner, which was, coincidentally that night. I didn't want to have to skip it (and I wouldn't have gone if I'd failed). I was a little tired, but I did pretty okay considering. It was a lot of fun. I finally met Ned Denison (he'd accused me of flirting with one of his favorite swimmers—the pretty one who'd given me directions), and had great conversations with a few amazing swimmers from past eras, Marilyn Bell especially.

We got more food from a grocery store on the way back. I was up nice and early the next morning and we went to the Catalina Swimming Association Brunch (I didn't realize it, but I was honored and spoke as one of the people who'd completed it that year). Cam's swim started Saturday night. Great conditions (and he'd improved a great deal in the preceding months). He easily beat my time and was well under 12 hours.

Everyone jumped in naked at the end of his swim (including me, and there were a couple of attractive women there). It was something that I wasn't excited to tell Sue about, but it wasn't actually about Sue—I'd felt weird about it. After I told her, I'd realized that it wasn't that she was going to be mad. She wasn't in the least—she laughed because she trusted me, and because she saw that it bothered me. I figured out that the simple question, "How would you tell your kids about it?" spoke volumes about why it was bothering me. I wasn't particularly worried about being naked around good looking women, I just realized that I was a bit old to be acting like an 18-year-old. The swimming, traveling, and mentoring are more appropriate ways for me to have fun.

Learning and Growing

I learned a lot from both Wild Sparks and from Catalina. If I wanted to be successful at any of my goals, I was going to have to work very hard, very smart, and make very good choices. I also learned that I could withstand failures, that I needed to learn from those failures, and that I still had a lot of growing to do.

The failures were teaching me a lot. Not just practical lessons (like about feeds and not ignoring the obvious signals I got from Marielle and Charlie), but about myself. About how to weather failure. About staying positive and taking the good things from every situation—wins or losses.

I still didn't know what I ultimately wanted to be doing, but during this time, as Innovation Labs was starting to really take shape, I started to figure out that I was meant to help people.

Tahoe in January

12 – Improving

2016 started well. The mass defection, Catalina, and Wild
Sparks were behind me. Morale was up. Cobaltix was doing
well. I was starting to see confluence, and Innovation Labs was
becoming fun. I had both confidence and was gaining focus.

Tahoe

January 31, 2016 marked the company trip to Tahoe. It was a chance for me to do something nice for people that work at Cobaltix. The crew that came up was younger—almost as much Innovation Labs as Cobaltix. Cam was up, too. He was skiing. I decided I wasn't going to ski, this close to the Irish Sea (less than 6 months out at that point). I'd also stopped playing water polo. I had a goal and getting injured would not have been a good thing.

This trip was important for me. In previous years, although it was always *my* trip, my old partner had always been the star of it. He's a great skier, and a very gregarious guy. I usually made the trip happen (at every level), but he somehow always managed to be the center of the attention. The 2015 trip had been a bust. There was no snow, but even more, there was no energy. I needed this to go well, even if just for me.

The first evening went very well. In the morning, I dropped everyone off at Homewood and headed over to a dock a few blocks away to jump in Lake Tahoe. After a quick chat with someone coming out to look at the view (it was beautiful), I got changed next to the car. Down to boots, a jacket, and carrying a towel, I walked over to the boat launch (much better than the rocky shoreline). I slipped on the ice as I was walking down and landed on my ass. Unhurt, I continued down to the water line where I shed my boots, towel, finally very warm jacket, and started walking into the water. It was cold. I knew I couldn't do a 10-minute entry like I usually do in the Bay. The ramp had some moss under water and was still slippery even after I was in the water, but there were no more mishaps. The water felt thicker. Within a minute, I was swimming.

It was cold. The water was 42F (5.5C) based on the NOAA buoy. I remember wondering if 42 degrees would count as an ice mile if I made it a mile. I've since checked and it has to be below 5C, but 42 degrees Fahrenheit is 5.5C. Quickly, though, my thought process changed. I was now thinking, what is the shortest distance I can swim. I needed to swim heads-up free because it hurt to put my face in the water. I swam out to a buoy about 50 yards (50m) away. I saw another buoy and went for it. By that point, I had my head down. It was butt-ass cold. I was a little out of breath but I was starting to settle down a bit. My hands and feet were completely numb as was all of the skin on my arms and legs. My face and body still seemed ok. I was realizing that my stroke was pretty clean—just no kick. My legs were just dragging behind me.

I swam back to the ramp where I started. As I approached, I decided that I was okay but that I was still going to stay pretty close. This was the coldest water I'd swum in since 1995 (1 mile or 1.6km at 37F/2.5C).

There were lots of buoys around. They were 35 to 55 yards (30-50m) apart, as close as I could tell. It took roughly a minute between each. I was swimming at normal speed, which surprised me. I was looking for any signs of core temperature drop (hypothermia) but found none. I was alert and everything was ok, except for the pain in my hands and feet from the cold. I blocked out the pain, though. My thinking was staccato but clear.

After a few more buoys, I figured I was at about 650 yards (600m). I pulled off my goggles and found a dock to shoot for. I headed about 300 yards (275m) away along the shoreline. The stop was less than 5 seconds. I went to the dock. The water was glass and the swim went quickly. As I got close, I took a few heads-up strokes. The water was cold and my hands were stiff.

I tried kicking and got little from the effort. I considered turning back to the launch, but I decided to go all the way to the next buoy. I estimated that I'd covered about 1200 yards (1100m) at that point. I turned back and headed along the shore. The water was clear and I could see every rock. I was moving well. My core was still ok.

I got to the dock and as I started to stand, I noticed a family with a couple of small kids. I had no problem talking to them. They didn't say much, but it was clear that the parents (younger than me) both thought I was crazy, and the looks on their faces told me they were thinking they were seeing something that they would never see again in their lifetimes. The kids wanted to swim. It just wasn't computing for them, snow and swimming.

I got out. No slips. Walking was fine, despite my feet being completely numb. I got dry, although I could not feel the towel on my skin. It was an odd dissociation seeing the towel touch my skin, but not feeling it, although I could feel a general burn starting. It was sunny. The air was probably about 40F (4.5C). I'm sure the sun didn't warm me much, but I doubt I would have gone as far or felt as brave had it been cloudy, even at the same air and water temperatures.

I put my boots and jacket on and went to the car. I had no problem handling the keys. I was thinking about taking a picture on my phone, but didn't at that point. As soon as the heater was warm, I took off my jacket and boots. I noticed that I'd left the passenger window open. It didn't matter much—the car was far warmer than the water had been.

After about 10 minutes (5 minutes in the car) I realized that the let-down was starting. That is when the blood begins flowing back to the skin and extremities (and cold blood starts back to the core). It happened pretty quickly. I never felt cold, but I know my core dropped a few degrees (about 1.5C) in just seconds. I was glad I was sitting down. I never felt bad or dizzy, but I know I wasn't far from it. For the first time in more than a year since Copenhagen, I felt cold. I shivered. I was laughing—it was such an odd feeling. I was thinking of one of the skinny guys at the club. Just ten degrees colder than the bay, and I was that guy that was cold and shivering.

I put the heater on my feet, too. I realized that as I was losing the numbness in my skin, my feet would start to hurt a lot. Warming them up faster would mean less time in that in-between painful state. I grabbed my phone and took a video-selfie so I could assess my shaking later. It was a really funny video—me shivering pretty hard and the camera shaking all over the place.

I was never in danger, but I was cold. I have the ability to hold onto the shunting for a while after I'm out of the water—long enough to dry off for sure. I doubt my core dropped even a degree in the water (in about 20 minutes), but it sure did when I got in the car. I wondered if the speed at which I warmed might have given rise to the shivering. I decided to try to warm slower next time.

I swam the next day with Cam and two others who jumped in as well. I went about the same distance as Saturday (about 1200 yards or 1300m over 20 minutes), but warmed up much more slowly. No shivering this time. Cam didn't make it quite as far, but he did a respectable 650 yards (600m).

The trip had turned out very well. The energy was great. The snow was great. The steaks were great. The whole weekend turned out great. In a small way, the morale of the company had gone up quite a bit, as had my confidence.

A Few Cold Swims

Cam has a pretty great training pattern. He drinks, stays out late, and generally has fun. Then about four or five months before a big event, he starts training very heavily, doing very long swims, back to back, sometimes even two long swims on the same weekend. He did a pair of 6-hour swims one weekend. The next weekend, did an 8-hour followed by 2 x 2-hour swims. I can't argue that this is a good way to prepare for a big swim, but I also can't do that.

I know that I need to recover between swims. I need to make sure I have long swims, but they have to come spaced apart. I want to spend as much time in really cold water as possible. Because I'm older, though, recovery is huge for me. I still need to train as many miles and as long as possible, but I can't do it all in just a few months before a swim. I also have to balance staying in cold water shape (and maintaining endurance) with dropping the long swims from my schedule with enough time to recover before a big swim.

To this end, I did a few swims in January when the water was cold. First was Airport (SFO) to the Golden Gate Bridge with the Locos. That was 5:15 at 49F (9.5C). That was a very good training swim for the Irish Sea, which I was expecting to be 54F (14C) over 14 hours. The second was my Irish Sea qualifier—7.5 hours, 49F (9.5C) for the first 6 hours, rising to 50-53F (10-11.5C) for the last 90 minutes. These, along with a few other shorter swims (3-5 hours) were to make up the bulk of my long training, with Catalina at the start and Juan de Fuca (a cold swim in June) capping my training at the end. My goal was to do as many cold long swims as possible, to have time to recover from each, and to be fully recovered by August for the Irish Sea.

Co-Conspirator

Just before Catalina, Cameron joined me in starting Cobaltix Compliance. It was a bit of a bet—definitely a risk. I was giving away a chunk of revenues from Cobaltix to fund Cobaltix Compliance, but I had a feeling about Cam. The feeling was that if I got him started right, if I gave him some training and just put him to work, that he'd not only do well, but would also be able to run Compliance.

Within a few months (by early 2016), there was more business than he could handle. We hired our first full-time employee in May, and about that time, another company came in interested in buying Cobaltix and Cobaltix Compliance. I pretty much immediately took Cobaltix off the table (even though the number was looking like more than 2x my number), but we continued to talk about the possibility of selling Compliance for a couple more weeks. The number we were talking about (a number we never agreed to) was very good, but I decided to stop the conversation. Business was just getting better and better and I didn't want to sell.

I snuck out to Chicago with Cam for a charity event (Cam runs a charity called Ubunye) and got in a good swim in Lake Michigan (15 minutes at 45F/7C) before the event. Then Sue and I brought Annika (and Kylie and Ethan) to visit East Coast schools and I got in a couple of swims in Boston (50 minutes at 46F/7.5C) and New York (25 minutes at 45F/7C).

While we were in Boston, I'd starting planning to do a swim from Canada to the US—Vancouver Island to Port Angeles, the Straights of Juan de Fuca. It would involve getting a special visa from Canada (a CANPASS); fortunately, my Global Entry card was all I needed on the US side.

Then we picked up a big client. It was a client for Compliance (doing data analysis), for SA935 (writing a new application), for Cobaltix (providing resources for them), and for Lighthouse— the new company formed by two of our former interns, Mikkel and Rune. Even the interns were finding great success, and I'd managed to invest a bit in them as well. The revenues and profits helped Compliance, SA935, and Lighthouse all turn the corner, although each was starting to do okay even before this client. I even got to swim in Newport when I visited the client.

I made it back to Ireland and Copenhagen in the Spring. Although I was sick for the first part of the trip, I got a lot done including recruiting a couple of interns and finding a good fellow.

Also, I'd swum with a great guy, Keith Garry, whom I'd met in San Francisco at the South End. He'd offered to put me up, and both he and his wife Oonagh (and their two boys) were incredibly nice. In the short time I was there, he also introduced me to his pilot Padriag, a great guy (and gave me Padraig's book to read). We'd swum twice in Carlingford (so beautiful) and had a great dinner with Padraig and Jacqueline (Padraig's girlfriend, and an ice-miler herself). Really fun, making such great friends, and they were so welcoming, warm, and things were really good. Business was good, and best of all doing good was good. I was starting to figure out some of the details around the helping people part, and the 100-year goal was starting to come a bit more into focus.

On the boat, just before leaving Vancouver Island

13 – Failure, Juan de Fuca

In April, I decided to add the swim across the Strait of Juan de Fuca to fill my dance card for 2016. It was meant as a short swim before the Irish Sea, to help with acclimatization—the water between Vancouver Island and Port Angeles, Washington is cold.

While very well trained for this swim, in the past two months, I'd realized that I'd signed up for something a little more than I'd bargained for.

Let me start from the beginning, though.

There is an annual 24-hour relay swim hosted by the Dolphin Club each year in the Bay. It attracts teams from all over the US, and sometimes even abroad. I haven't done it (it is hard to fit in because it requires you to be at the club for 24 straight hours, and you don't get much sleep. Each person on the team of six swims 4 hours total, an hour in followed by a 5-hour break. Some teams only have 4 or 5 people, but the concept is the same. It is a cold-water swim (52F/11C is pretty normal), so doing 4 legs over a night is pretty hard for a lot of people.

It was there that I met Andrew Malinak. That night I swam with a few people—I needed to get in 5 hours that night, so I did buddy swims with a bunch of people who were less acclimated than me. It was fun supporting other people. I swam with Andrew for one of those hours, and we ended up talking afterward. His girlfriend Erika was there, too.

He said I should come up and swim from Vancouver Island, BC to Port Angeles, WA—the Juan de Fuca Straight. I was instantly interested—one country to another...cool. Water was cold...check. Not short...good. So, I called him and we started setting it up. I learned it would be around 49F (9.5C). Then I found out it had an 85% failure rate, and only 8 people had done it. Awesome. It was a little longer than I'd though, too—almost 14 miles (22km). Currents were a little tricky, too. Weather was not easy to predict (like the English Channel).

Now I've got a very real swim in the beginning of June (thank god Andrew had talked me out of a May date and colder water). As May was going by, training was going well. I had got a short taper planned, and I start to think about my very cool swim (pun intended). I started to realize that this wasn't going to be easy like Gibraltar—this could be more like English Channel hard. Potentially 7 hours at 48 or 49 (9-9.5C) is something to start worrying about.

I did do two 49F (9.5C) swims in January (the 5.5-hour and 6 of the 7.5-hour, it warmed up a few degrees toward the end). In theory I should be able to do this, but the water in the Bay had gotten to 58 degrees (14.5C) by the end of May. My anxiety had started rising. What if the currents make it an 8 hour, or even longer swim?

Work was a little busy the last couple of weeks before the swim. I managed good training, but my stress level was a bit high. Mostly good problems, but still stress. Less sleep. Construction at the house was going full bore. A lot more stress. We didn't have a landscaper (the one we had, completely failed). The one good thing was that swimming was going well. Shoulders were doing well, and my training was right on plan. My recovery from my 7.5-hour swim was good...about 2 weeks.

The day arrives, flight takes off at 7pm. At 5pm at the office in San Francisco, I noticed that the flight was leaving from Oakland...damn. I made it (with time to spare; the flight was late), but just a little more stress. When I got to SEATAC, though, the stress began to melt. The woman behind the Alamo rental counter asked me what I was doing in Seattle. Just an innocent question. A question I've answered with calculated bravado and modesty many times in the past few months, depending on the person asking it.

But with her, although the words I answered with were a variation on the same phrase I'd used many times ("I'm going to try to swim from British Columbia to Port Angeles.") somehow my voice was quite different. I knew I was going to try, and try hard, but I'm sure she could tell that success was far from certain in my mind. She asked a lot of questions. This was her story for the night. She upgraded me to a nice Audi for almost nothing. Things were going well, but I was not exactly exploding with confidence.

The false bravado was gone now. It was me and the strait. I suddenly started to think about the next few days, really think about them, as I drove up past Sequim (pronounced SKWIM) to Port Angeles in the dark as midnight rolled by.

Chilling Out

I got checked in around 1:30am and woke up early (longer days that far north). I read for a little bit, hoping to fall back to sleep, but the brightness outside was not going to let that happen. So, I loaded up my bag, and took off driving. The plan developed as I went. This area was truly beautiful.

I drove for about 35 minutes, following the line of where I might end up at the end of the swim (being washed toward the Pacific for most of the swim as I aimed directly across). I stopped the car about where I thought I'd probably land, at Salt Creek Recreation Area, in Tongue Point Sanctuary. I parked and changed, then walked down to the water at end of the tide pools where the beach started. I climbed in. Cold.

It was colder than 49 (9C) all right. The NOAA buoy had said 48.9 (9.4C) when I checked a few days before. It was supposed to get warmer in June. I was cold at first, but adjusted and swam well. I swam to Port Crescent about 1.3 miles (2.1km) away. I measured the distance later. On the way over, I saw a nice eatin' crab (Dungeness, just the right size). I dove down to it—about 7 feet (2m) down, but decided not to touch it as it ran away from me on the bottom.

I was doing pretty okay. The water was glass, sky overcast. No wind to speak of. There were a lot of people there. It was funny that no one talked to me even though everyone was looking at me...some were even pointing. I took one feed (and a bar just before). I felt good getting out, but cold...not really shivering, although just on the verge. I walked back to the car (farther than I'd remembered) and got my clothes from the trunk. When I was sure I was good (and not going to start shivering hard), I took off.

About 20 minutes away, I found a place that said, "Breakfast all day," and went in (towel around my waist, jacket on) and ordered 5 eggs scrambled with cheese and 8 pieces of bacon with decaf. It was waiting for me when I got back from the bathroom. I ate it and drank the coffee (many cups) as I warmed up, and then started working.

About 3 hours later, I was starting to get ready to leave when I got a call from a Washington state number. I picked it up. It was the hotel. Someone had found my wallet where I'd parked for my swim. I immediately asked the waitress if I could pay later, and started to the car. In the car, I called the number I was given, and offered to do whatever was most convenient to get it back. The guy was incredibly nice. He said he was coming this way anyway with his son, and he'd drop it off. So, I went back in and took my computer back out after explaining what was going on to the extremely nice and patient waitress. In my head, I was sure this guy would never take a reward, but I'd figured I could give it to his son.

About 10 minutes later, a guy about my dad's age and a younger guy (maybe 30) walked in. He walked right up to me, and said, "Steve?" Only later did it occur to me that he'd seen my driver's license picture. Although I did offer, they wouldn't accept a reward, I talked to them for a little bit. I told them about the swim and asked them about their plans (and for once probably listened a lot more than I talked). When they were leaving, I said that I would pay it forward. That made them both quite happy. They were really great people.

I finished the work I was doing. Then I went to pay the bill. I figured, "Why not make good on my promise right now?" The waitress had already left, but she'd been quite kind. I gave instructions to the new waitress that I was leaving a $100 bill as a tip (on $17 breakfast). As I was walking out the door, Kylee (the new waitress, like my daughter Kylie) was calling my waitress. I heard Kylee say, "You're not crying are you?" She was. I'd done a good thing.

Two days before the swim, positive things were happening. I'd gone from hubris to humility, and a couple of people's lives were better because I dropped my wallet (I could tell this was the highlight of the day for the father and son—they were just that kind of good people).

I do have to say where I had dinner. One of the best meals I've had anywhere. Woodfire Grill in Port Angeles. Meat was cooked perfectly. I told the chef and owner (they were standing next to each other in the kitchen) that you could cut the meat with paper—that tender. I had a beef short rib and also tenderloin medallions (two dinners, and yes it was good). If anyone reading this ever does this swim, go there.

The next day, I woke up early again and went down to Sequim, to the harbor I was thinking the boat would be at (I think there's only one). I got in and swam around. I guessed it was 53F (11.5C) when I got in (shallow, warmer) and got down to 49 (9.5C). I swam 30 minutes, about a mile, without a cap. I had a bit of a sore throat, but it wasn't bothering me at all in the water. I got some stuff at Walmart (including some lozenges) and just took care of stuff generally, then took a short nap.

I met Scott, Andrew, and Erika at the hotel (they arrived around 5:30pm). I remember talking to Scott, and I said I'd never not finished a swim. We went back to the Woodfire Grill again. It was even better the second time with good company.

Charles (the pilot) was very worried about conditions. Andrew calmed him down over the phone during dinner, and we agreed that Thursday was still the best day.

I went to bed at around 10:30pm and woke up at 4am (a little early). I had to start heating the drinks for the swim.

Damn Cold

For starters, I was wrong about the temperature, when I'd been swimming the previous two days. It felt colder because it was colder. It was 46F in the straight.

Here's a quick spoiler—I've now not finished a swim.

Everything leading up went exactly as planned. We found Charles, the pilot. He was wearing a uniform. He had been a computer guy in his previous life. This was his retirement. Nice guy, if a bit precise (not a bad trait for the pilot of the swim).

We got on and started out toward Canada. I had a PowerCrunch bar. It took a couple of hours to get to Canada from Sequim. Andrew checked in with the Canadian Government (we all had CANPASSes). It was cool crossing into Canadian waters. I sent Sue a couple of texts with pictures. About 30 minutes out, I had another PowerCrunch bar. All according to plan.

When we got to the shore, it was absolutely beautiful. We had about 45 minutes. We decided to leave about 30 minutes early based on where the current line was (a bit into the strait, but moving toward us). The water was pretty flat. A perfect day. Wind was light at 5 knots or less.

It took about 5 minutes to get ready and lube my chafe-points. Another 5 minutes procrastinating, then I dove in and swam to the rocks. It was cold. It felt warm when I got out, but I just dismissed that and swam back out through the shore kelp.

For the first three hours, I fed about every 30 minutes (just one at 45 minutes). When I got in, I was not confident that I'd make it, but it wasn't my mind that stopped me. The first three hours were just cold. I did okay in general. Although my hands and feet hurt, I was doing well. Feeds were well under 30 seconds (probably averaging about 20). Sun was out. My stroke count was very high for me, averaging around 72. I'm usually around 58. I think it was just so I could keep my core temperature up. I was pushing a lot of water and moving at a fast clip (23 minute miles).

Sometime after 3 hours, my arms started hurting. They weren't sore and it wasn't my shoulders, but my arms just weren't responding very well. My mind was alert and the noise was not a problem. I was okay mentally, so I just pushed harder. A little while later, maybe around 3.5 hours, I realized that I couldn't eat or drink. My stomach wasn't upset and I wasn't sea sick or sick at all; my stomach was just no longer working. I took about 3 oz of liquid (warm 50/50 Snapple), which ended up being my last real feed.

At about 4 hours, I felt pain in my lower back. Not muscle pain, but a deep pointed pain in the same place on both sides. After a few minutes, I realized that my kidneys were shutting down. Sue had texted "Swim, you bastard, swim!" That made me smile and carried me through the next 10-15 minutes.

Then the pain in my arms came back. It had never really left, but I was just noticing it much more. It was centered on my forearms and wrists (my hands had been fixed and not really movable for more than an hour, but I'd just ignored that). About the same time, my legs started seizing. It was coming from the top front of my thighs near my pelvis from deep inside. It wasn't just cramping…this was much different.

I tried to stretch out with some backstroke but realized I wasn't moving forward. I took a feed at 4:23 (spilled most of the 2-3 oz. because of the shivering) and did a little breaststroke (more like ineffective sculling). My teeth were chattering and in the couple of minutes that had passed, I was now shivering. My limbs hurt. They weren't sore; it was a deeper pain.

I took a few strokes of free and realized that my arms and legs just weren't responding. I was pretty spastic at this point. It wasn't a matter of just telling my arms and legs to do something, my forearms were seized and my upper and lower legs were cramping and spasming. I was even starting to lose control of my core muscles. Within seconds I went to shivering uncontrollably and my teeth started chattering so much that my neck hurt. I was all done.

Once I got back in the boat, Scott told me how cold it was.

I do wish I'd finished, but I was actually quite happy with the swim. 4:26 mostly at 46.0F (7.7C). It was more than I would have expected I was capable of. I will be back to do this again—hopefully at more like 48-49F (9-9.5C).

I covered 10.8 miles (17.4km), left 3 miles (5km) on the table. I was probably 2 hours from finishing as the tide was moving me quickly toward the Pacific, not toward shore (assuming that I would have made it in).

When I got back on the boat, my core started warming up immediately. The boat was protected from the wind, and so I tried something that had been working well to that point—warming up slowly (like over a half an hour). "The drop" comes when you warm up your skin. Your body feels it is safe, and stops shunting blood away from the skin. The skin is still cold, though, and the blood from the skin causes the core temperature to drop. I was going to do it slowly.

I drip dried over about 3-4 minutes. Then I got a towel and dried off for a few more minutes. My skin was cold (maybe 50F/10C) but it was slowly warming up. I was still shivering at this point, but my teeth stopped chattering as soon as I was out of the water. I then put on a pair of light pants; next was shoes and socks, then a short sleeve shirt. All this was over about 15 minutes. I was still cold, but no longer shivering. I guessed my core temp was around 94F (35C) by that point. Then I put on a sweatshirt. My skin was slowly coming back up from what was probably around 50F/10C, and by the time I got my jacket on (after about 25 minutes), my core temperature was getting closer to normal (about 96F/36C).

When we got back to Port Angeles about an hour after the swim, my hands and feet still felt cold, but I was warm. I was still wearing the jacket, but it came off about 20 minutes later. I felt a little cold (both chilled and like I had a cold) for the next few hours. The head cold came on in full force that night. I didn't sleep at all between twitching and the head cold. The head cold lasted about 3 days. I don't think the swim helped, but I think I had it before the swim.

On the boat, Scott had said, "The Irish Sea will be 8 degrees (4.5C) warmer." That made me smile. I was back to normal (a relative term when describing me) about an hour after we got back. My feet were cold for a couple of hours, but I warmed up slowly and effectively. I was shivering when I got out of the water (I don't shiver often), but that only lasted about 15-20 minutes.

On the way in, we had to check in with the Coast Guard. Andrew had alerted a local paper, there was a reporter there with a photographer. There were two brief articles on the swim (one that I was going to do it, another that I'd failed). Also, Steve Munatones published a couple of articles on the web as well. A lot of publicity for a failure.

A few days later, there were no lingering effects. The cold passed and I was a little tired from the swim, but I was never in any danger. I was alert and completely cognitive the whole time. My brain was slowly turning off the least important things, and I made a good decision to get out when I did.

I'm glad I pushed it that far. Also, glad I didn't push it farther. I now have a limit. I'm not thinking that training or acclimatization will help me go much further than 4.5 hours at 46.0F/7.7C. I was working hard the whole way. It's not likely I could have generated more heat.

After the swim, we packed up and drove to Bainbridge. It was a long drive for me even though it was only a couple of actual hours. I met the team at the Harbor Public House. There were a bunch of swimmers there from the local Masters team. They all congratulated me (on a failed swim) and paid for our drinks. Also, I'd heard that I'd been a story on one of the Seattle TV stations. It must have been a very slow day. Finally, I met a friend of Scott's (Candace) who offered to put me up for the night on her couch. It was so generous of her. I couldn't have made it to a hotel at that point. I have to say that I owe her, probably more than she'll ever know.

I have to think about this swim in other terms. I found out later, it turned out to be one of the coldest distance swims ever done. Records are not good enough to say that it was a world record. I swam 10.8 miles (17.4km) in 4:26 mostly at 46.0 degrees (7.7C). There have been very few distance swims at or below 49 degrees (9.5C). In asking knowledgeable people, I have only found two similarly cold swims. Both that were much longer, but both were also likely closer to 49F (9.5C) than 46F. Not bad for a failure. Probably a "world best."

In looking at goals and failure, I have one data point that seems somewhat similar. We have tried to make a difference in Haiti with Zanmi Lakay. It has been hard. I don't think that we've made a lasting difference that will help future generations, but even in failing we've made a small difference to a handful of kids. They know someone cares and I hope they might have even learned something that will help them in the future. I hope to do better than this, but Jen and Guy Pantaleon each said something to me, "It would be great to make a huge difference, but if failing is making these kids feel good about themselves, like someone cares about them, even just for a couple of weeks a year, I'll take failing over not trying."

The swim was a failure in the sense that I didn't get to the other side but in another sense, it was good. In trying for something lofty (or at least something very hard to do), I achieved something else. It wasn't as good as finishing, but it was still good. It was a good training swim for the Irish Sea.

It always helps to always look at the positives. There were a lot here.

When you set outrageous goals, failure can actually end up being good.

Seven weeks to the Irish Sea!

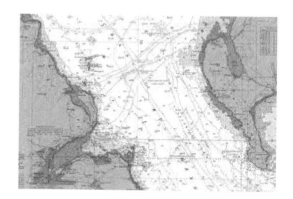

Ireland to Scotland

14 – Ireland

I left San Francisco on August 1st. I'd been bragging to everyone that I was going to attempt to swim the Irish Sea, or was going to swim from Ireland to Scotland, or some similar variation depending on who I was talking to. The last couple of weeks before were hard. I was nervous. I was not feeling confident, which probably explains all the posturing, bragging...whatever it was that I was doing.

After Juan de Fuca, the plan was to swim hard for about 5 weeks. The first couple of weeks were good. I'd done quite a bit of distance (in the water 11 days of the 2 weeks), and managed to get in a 4-hour and two 5-hour swims. Then I had a week that was a little slower, four days in the water and not so much distance. I followed that with two good weeks, again 11 days in 14, averaging over 10km a workout (6+ miles). I was getting into good shape again. Between the cold from Juan de Fuca and the hard training of the 5 weeks after, I was getting to a very good place. It was probably 60F/15.5C in the Bay at that point in July, which wasn't so good (was I losing my acclimatization?), but my weight was slowly climbing. I was at 207 lbs (94 kg.).

My wedding weight had been 192 (87 kg.) and my English Channel weight had been 243 (110 kg.). The heaviest I got before I quit carbs was 247 (112 kg.). Being at 207 (94 kg.) was probably not a bad weight to be at given the cold of the Irish Sea. Maybe even a couple more pounds (a kilo) would be good. I just knew that I'd have to lose it (slowly) after I got back and I wasn't looking forward to weeks of eating carefully. Steaks and bacon are good.

After the 5 hard weeks, I was supposed to taper (the plan was 3 weeks of taper, or slowly easing up to rest for the event). But I was already starting to second guess my strategy. I started to realize that I might have started my taper too early. I was starting to feel good and rested, and I still had a week before I left for Ireland, a week after that in Ireland, and maybe more if I didn't swim on the first day of the window. I decided to drop a couple of 2-plus-hour swims in before I left and also started swimming without a cap to try to counter-balance the fact that the Bay was getting warmer.

Cameron got back after his successful Irish Sea swim (about 12.5 hours, 54F/12C), and let me know that the only issue with his swim was the cold, and even that wasn't so bad. He'd assured me that I'd have no issues and even that the jellies were not as bad as we'd been worrying about. Andrew McLaughlin (another South Ender and Loco) had more trouble with the swim, but he'd finished, too in a little over 14 hours. That was good to hear, but my anxiety level was still rising.

The kids had water polo Junior Olympics in San Jose (successive weekends) in the 10 days before I was leaving, so I drove down to Santa Cruz to get water that was just a little colder (more like 56F/13.5C). I did 5 workouts down there in the last 12 days before I left (plus 6 more in the Bay), even doing a 2-hour swim in Santa Cruz, as well.

I was feeling good physically, but not mentally. I was starting to feel like I had built everything up so much and that I was going to fail. I was regretting having told anyone, even Sue and my parents not to mention everyone at the club. I wished I could have done it like Gibraltar. Only a handful of people knew what I was up to back then. Now everyone knows I'm not only shooting for the North Channel, but also the remainder of the Oceans7, too. Not finishing this would be disastrous, especially after failing at Juan de Fuca (notwithstanding the 46F/7C temp).

A little part of my brain knows that this anxiety is normal during a taper, but that little part of my brain was keeping quiet.

On Monday, August 1st, the plan was to get a quick swim in, then head to work before catching the flight out. I didn't manage to get the swim in but instead brought Ethan straight to work with me. We headed out on the 5:30pm flight to Dublin.

Sue and I had decided that I'd bring Ethan with me, and she'd follow with the girls closer to the first day of the swim. Planning had proven difficult, though, and they were to arrive on the first day of the window, which meant that they needed a car in case they arrived after I was in the water. I was looking forward to hanging out with Ethan, actually doing stuff that was fun for him with very little work to interfere.

On that first day (Tuesday), after driving up from Dublin to Belfast (Helen's Bay), I was still thinking I had overdone my taper, I swam as soon as I got there. The water was a bit cold (probably 54F/12C), but not too bad. I did an hour in Ballyholme. I got up early on Wednesday (now 6 days before my swim window was to open) and swam with someone Keith had connected me with who was preparing for the swim also— Shubham Vanmali from India.

On Wednesday evening, we swam with some friends of Oonagh's for an hour (Oonagh is Keith's wife, who plays water polo; her name is pronounced "Una"). We swam about an hour north of Belfast, where the water was supposedly colder (although it felt the same or warmer to me). We swam with Nuala and Ruth and a couple of nice teenage girls who were all Oonagh's water polo team. They were preparing for a North Channel relay themselves. They were incredibly nice people, warm, not too fast (Shubham and I messed around a lot, marinating).

On Thursday morning, I swam with Ethan (yes, he got in, too!) in Helen's Bay, just a quick 30 minutes. The water was a short walk from the Bridge House B&B.

On my last visit to Europe, I'd met 3 "Lads" (Fionn, Eoin, and Chris who were all 18-19 years old) who had a company and were now dropping out of school to make a god of it. They were going to do very well. I'd brought Chris Kelly to San Francisco for a month in the fellowship program, so that gave us a good excuse to see another part of Ireland.

In Limerick (at the University of Limerick, UL), I did a very mini version of shark tank for some of the more promising entrepreneurs in the incubation lab where Chris and the lads were working. The entrepreneurs had some interesting ideas, but all needed a bit of guidance on the business and finance side of things. That was how Chris wanted to use me. It was actually quite fun. Afterwards, we popped over to the UL rowing club and I swam for about 45 minutes in the Shannon River. It was okay, appeared to be clean (even though it was right below a sewage treatment plant). The water was a little warmer, maybe 57F (14C), but it was fresh, which always feels colder. I didn't swim terribly long; about 1.5 miles (2.5km).

That night we went to dinner with Chris's parents (who are near my age, very nice). At one point, I went to the bathroom, and I remember thinking as I looked at my bearded face in the mirror, if my son brought me home, I would be scared.

The next morning, Chris and Ethan flew a drone (this was the older model of the two the lads had). We met his cousins (who had just returned from a decade in Mountain View, CA). Then, Chris did something completely unexpected. He gave Ethan the drone. It was both incredibly generous and also very well received. We then took a trip to a castle before heading to the incubation lab to talk more.

We had a few more conversations in the morning and early afternoon (while Ethan flew the drone), then we drove back toward Belfast, stopping briefly to swim in Carlingford (a beautiful place about an hour north of Dublin) for just a quick 1.2-mile (2km) swim, about 40 minutes. The water was still hovering around 54F (14C).

Shubham Vanmali is 20. The word kid doesn't fit him, though. He swam the English Channel at 18 and since had completed Catalina and Gibraltar (meaning as we were training, he was tied with me and just one behind Cameron for the Oceans7). As we were training in Ireland, Keith was just a bit faster than Shubham, who was just a hair faster than me. The thing that impressed me the most about him, though, was his maturity. He was comfortable with anyone and had an outlook on life that was far beyond his years. I was enjoying swimming with him.

We'd also met a guy named Attila Mányoki who was also going for the Oceans7 and was fresh off of having set the Molokai record (28 miles/43km). He hadn't done Gibraltar yet. Attila is a bit brash and doesn't hesitate to tell anyone who will listen that he intends to set the record in every swim he attempts. At first, his bravado put me off, but over time, he grew on me a bit.

After swimming with Attila and hearing about his preparation, I thought his setting the record would be a longshot and his finishing was nearly as questionable. I know that I cannot see into a person's heart, though I can't see their toughness.

Attila could go a long ways (I'd learned his longest swim was 85km) and the Molokai record is not something to be scoffed at. But it didn't seem like he was in the right frame of mind and he wasn't well adjusted to the cold. Keith, Shubham, and Attila were not as thick as me. Attila, though, would get out after an hour and he would be shivering. He'd go straight for the car heater (not like Keith, Shubham, or me). He just didn't seem to be there yet. Also, he was heavily sponsored in Hungry. I've noticed that money in this sport seems to create bad endings.

Windows and Pilots

A window is the period when the tides are favorable, usually the neap tide, when the moon is neither full nor new. A neap tide means less tide differential and easier to predict tidal flows near the shores, which is important in most channel swims. In many channels it is unlikely that someone could make it across during a spring tide. The North Channel is one of those places.

Which spot you have in a window is also very important. You arrange for it at least a year in advance. With three pilots, there are three spots per good day in any given window. In the August window, I had the first spot, and Attila was to go behind me in the second spot with Quinton Nelson piloting. Phia Steyn (a South African, by way of Scotland) was to go first with Shubham in the second spot with Brian Meharg as the pilot. Keith was to go with Padraig. Behind Keith with Padraig was a guy named Xarris Theodosis (pronounced Harris) from Greece.

We met Xarris just before the swim. He and his crew were incredibly nice. Padraig had found another boat, and was going to Pilot Keith, but navigate for both swimmers. This wasn't conventional, but was not a bad idea.

Probably worth making a note about the pilots. Quinton Nelson and Brian Maharg are great guys and incredibly experienced pilots. Both are very invested in each swim and swimmer. Although quite different from each other, they share a great deal of knowledge about the tides, conditions, weather, course, and swimming (although neither are swimmers themselves). Quinton is a bit more reserved but has the best success record on the NC. Brian is a bit more animated and has a very similar record.

The third pilot is a newcomer, an experienced swimmer, Padraig Mallon. Padraig is the least experienced seaman, but make no mistake, he is quite qualified and is starting to take the reins as the most sought after pilot as Quinton and Brian get close to retiring (both are in their 70s). Padraig has a book is fun to read, too. He runs a camp for swimmers at the beginning of the summer. Andrew McLaughlin credits this camp with part of his success, and I think he's correct.

Padraig is truly a cold-water ultra-marathon swimmer and advocate of the sport. His swims include the EC, NC, ice mile, and many other crazy exploits. He has more than enough personality to fill a room and won't hesitate to tell you if he thinks you're wrong (but he does listen, too). He's a great guy.

You can't go wrong with any of the three pilots, and probably the best approach is to talk to all three, if you have a choice. The most important thing will be getting your deposit in to get the first spot in your window. There was only one swimmable day in my window, sometimes there aren't any. If you're attempting the NC, you want to have the first slot in your window. As you'll see, this is incredibly important in all swims, but especially in the NC.

Cushendun, Cushendall, and Crew

On Saturday, we went north to Cushendun and met Keith, Oonagh, and their two boys (7 and 8) and a friend and her two kids. The swim was about an hour. I went no cap the last 25 minutes. After the swim (where Keith got a little stung on the face –probably by a Compass), we got back and got Ethan's drone out of a tree (no mean feat). It was actually pretty fun. I climbed up and Keith and I brainstormed. He's a hair quicker to try things (which I like). We both think alike. You won't know until you try. He's also very good at assessing risk. He owns a recruiting business in the aircraft space.

After we got the drone out of the tree, we all headed to Cushendall where we went to a mini-life-saving fair (with a mechanical bull and a rock wall for the kids). It was a ton of fun, even if just an hour. Then we picked up some wetsuits from a friend of Keith's, headed up the coast about an hour further, and went cliff diving. The cliffs started at about 1m (3ft), and moved up gradually to about 6m+ (20ft). It was a ton of fun.

We left toward the end of the day, heading back to Helen's Bay, grabbing a quick dinner before heading to bed.

On Sunday, after a quick 30-minute swim in Crawfordsburn, we headed to Donegal and Ballyshannon (where Sarah and Brian live). I bought Sue a nice Barber coat (something she's wanted for a long time, since it was our anniversary) in Donegal. Then we met Sarah and Brian. Sarah and Brian and I talked through feeds. Brian's wife Marcella and daughter Amy talked to Ethan. I'd met Brian on a previous trip to see Sarah but just quickly swam with him that time. He was incredibly nice, easy to talk to, and such a positive person. He and Sarah would make up the core of my crew along with someone Donal Buckley had recommended—Owen O'Keefe. Sarah was the exact person I wanted to lead my crew, and as it turned out Brian was equally good. Owen turned out to be good, too—almost better for Sarah and Brian than for me (having swum the English Channel). All three were an incredibly positive force on the boat. What an incredible team. I was lucky to have them especially given that I was coming from a continent away.

These two days, with these people, brought many thoughts together in my mind. Here were four people, Keith, Oonagh, Sarah, and Brian, who were not only helping me, but taking time out to be especially nice to Ethan, too. None of them had any reason to do it—nothing to gain. Yet, here they were helping me, opening their houses, their days, and their minds to me. They introduced me to people who were similarly generous. They gave me confidence and made me feel good.

I realized that I wanted to be like them. Not just that I wanted to pay the favors forward, but that I wanted to be like them.

This was something that I would spend all of my free cycles thinking about. How I could do what they do, to be more like them? How would this dovetail into my plans, and what it would mean for Innovation Labs and for my 100-year goal?

False Start

On Monday, I got word that I might be swimming Wednesday, the second day of my window. I swam about 50 minutes with Attila and Shubham (no cap) in Donaghadee. I also got nailed pretty good by a big compass jellyfish. It wasn't the worst thing ever, but it was painful for a day, then itched like crazy for another. Although I wasn't taking it as a bad sign, it wasn't so great either. I took prednisone and alternately applied Benadryl and hydrocortisone. I also took a couple of Benadryl, then a couple more later that evening. Two did nothing, four seemed to work a lot better. I didn't want to heavily drug myself, but I knew I was going to have a lot of trouble sleeping without antihistamine to knock me out and keep me from scratching.

The weather was pretty dicey, but it seemed like there might have been a one-day gap between two low-pressure systems that were spinning off the high-pressure system southwest of Ireland in the Atlantic. The weather in the NC is even worse than the weather in the English Channel. It is up to each swimmer to decide when they go, with advice from their pilot and/or crew, once they are at their spot in their window. Sometimes it isn't much of a choice. You go on a good day. Other times, though, the decision can be very complex, taking into account your spot in the window, other possible days, how long you've been waiting (the neap usually only lasts 4-8 days), whether you're ready, crew commitments, and not least of all, the weather forecast for both your day, and the prospects of a good day or days later in the window.

I got everyone alerted on Monday night and began the 24-hour countdown. There is a ton to do: get food for the crew, prep feeds, contact crew, watch the BBC weather on the Internet, and watch WindGuru. Not to mention, communicating with the pilot, finalizing the jump time, preparing the grease, packing, planning the pre-jump timeline, and getting to bed on time. All of this while resting, relaxing, and getting in a quick 25-minute loosen-up swim. I got everything done and although Keith and Padraig had advised me that the weather was going to be far better on the weekend, I was prepared to go...probably not ready mentally, but that would come once I knew for sure we were going.

On Tuesday morning, I swam a half hour without a cap in Ballyholme with Shubham, then Ethan and I went to pick up Sue and the girls. We got back about 6 hours later. I was getting ready psychologically. I had to be positive. If this was the best day in the window, I didn't just want to "make the best of it." I'd never make it with that attitude. I had to truly believe that I'd make it no matter what. I was in that mind-set.

By Tuesday afternoon, the weather was looking dubious at best. After talking to Keith and Padraig, I called Quinton, and we decided to wait.

This decision would also have a ramification for Attila. Me not swimming Wednesday meant that I would likely swim Sunday. He would have to choose between Saturday and Monday. The weather did not look good after Monday for a week (well into the Spring tide and the more unpredictable currents). With him in the second position, I would choose my day first, and he would then choose the next best day.

I didn't have to decide yet, but I would have to decide tentatively by Thursday night to be fair to Attila, and stick to my decision unless the weather changed. If I chose Sunday, but it turned out to be windy, I could still choose Monday, but I couldn't just change on a whim once I'd put in dibs for my day.

It turned out that not going on Wednesday was good. The day started off good as WindGuru predicted, but by the afternoon it was blowing hard (25+ knots). I never would have made it.

On Wednesday, I swam in the morning at Ballyholme. I went about 2 miles at 24-minute pace (pretty fast) without a cap. I was easily keeping up Shubham this day. My taper was coming together well.

After swimming, we went over to Ballyshannon again. We went into Donegal for a quick visit. Sue exchanged the jacket I'd gotten her for the right size.

Brian had set up the kids for surfing (including his daughter Amy). Brian had a wedding to go to on Saturday and Sarah was supposed to work on Monday. Also, Owen was not available on Saturday. That meant that for the crew, Sunday was the best. I couldn't decide based on them (as long as I had one person, I could do it), but the best day for them, by far, would be Sunday.

When we got to Ballyshannon, the kids surfed (Sarah boogie boarded), and Brian, Marcella (his wife), and I swam about a mile, about 30 minutes, nice and easy in good 4 to 5-foot (1.5m) surf. When I got out, Sue had taken a walk on the beach. Ordinarily, I would have been quite happy that she was enjoying herself, but she had the keys to the car and my clothes were locked in the car. Sarah and Brian were quite concerned, but I was able to walk around in a speedo with no problems for 45 minutes. The wind was gusting to 45-50 knots and it was cold, but I was fine. It did take me a while to warm up, but my acclimatization was proving to be good.

We all had a great lunch with Brian, Amy, and Marcella. I didn't manage to pay for the wetsuits and surfboards, but I did manage to pick up lunch. The crew is kind of like a wedding party...if the swimmer can afford it, they should pick up the expenses, as much as possible, for the crew.

Assuming Sunday, I now had 3 days to get mentally ready.

On Thursday, I swam 45 minutes, alternating slow and fast.

After breakfast (still the best anywhere), we visited the Titanic museum. It was a very good, well-curated experience. After that, we ate in Belfast, did a little shopping, and played Ping-Pong. Shubham joined us for all this. We had a lot of fun. I got a bunch of walking in. There'd be no real walking Friday or Saturday so I could rest.

Friday, I swam with Attila and Shubham. We did a very short swim, 20 minutes. Phia joined us as well. She was slow but quite comfortable in the cold. I didn't think she would make it, although I thought she would be able to last a long time. I also thought she was a bit weird, kind of like all of us, but I couldn't really fit her into a box. I later found out she was an academic (African studies of some sort or another), which partially explained things. She wasn't not nice, but I just didn't connect with her on that Friday. I suspect part of it might have been that she was nervous, although she didn't seem so.

In the afternoon, I confirmed Sunday (it was a foregone conclusion). The weather was likely to be very good on Sunday, but marginal on Saturday with high winds predicted for Monday.

On Friday evening, Keith and I swam in Carlingford for about 25 minutes, and we all went to dinner. I did get a chance to treat him to a nice meal. It was probably still not nearly enough to pay him back for the incredible time I'd had with them and Ethan in Cushendun, or for hosting me in April, but it was a very good meal. The kids had a lot of fun.

Attila and Shubham were to attempt on Saturday. I'd wished them both good luck on Friday by email. It was their time and they needed to be in their heads. I would have loved to have gone down to wish them both off, but I wasn't sure I'd see them and they were already set to go.

There'd been a scare with Shubham. His crew had bailed on him when he didn't swim in the first 4 days of the window. He'd managed to get another guy to crew, but that guy bailed on him at the last minute, too, which turned out to be far best. While we were at dinner with Keith and his family on Friday, we got the word that he was without a crew.

I called Owen to see if he could go Saturday with Shubham instead of me, but he couldn't. Oonagh and Keith called Ruth (water polo, who we swam with a week before). Although she had just arrived on her vacation in Donegal (2.5 hours away), she packed up and turned around to crew for him. What's more, she put him up for weeks afterward, too. Ruth is one of the nicest people I know, right up there with Keith, Oonagh, Sarah, and Brian.

After breakfast (and upon finding about 20 signs from the proprietors saying, "You can. You will."), I got in a quick swim in Helen's Bay. It was nice. The weather was good and I had hopes that Attila and especially Shubham would have a good day. We went to the Ulster Folk Museum, a collection of buildings and a working farm from the 1914 era. Nearby was a transportation museum that we checked out, too. I snuck off for a nap in the car and slept for about an hour at one point. During the day, I did a little more shopping, packed, set down the timeline, and just generally checked items off the list. Sarah and Cillian (her youngest son, 12) arrived late in the afternoon. I confirmed the time with Quinton (he pushed the jump time back 30 minutes), made up the grease, and then we had pizza and middle-eastern food for dinner. I ate lightly and had some yogurt for dessert. Then Sarah and I did the final packing so she would know exactly what I had. It was funny but everything I was packing was for her to take care of me with. All I had to think about was my suit, cap, and goggles. That was all I'd be crossing with.

In the evening I heard from Keith (just before Oonagh took away his devices) that neither Attila nor Shubham had made it. I didn't have any details, just something about Attila and a seizure.

Steve Walker

Departing Donaghadee, with channel grease and beard.

15 – Swimming The Irish Sea

I got up at 4:30am. I had a PowerCrunch bar and a small yogurt. I drank a caffeine-free diet coke—all as per my usual ritual. I had another bar at 6:30am.

' the bags with Sarah into the car. Sue got the kids
ciating Sue. She was absolutely awesome. She
.ɔcɑɪbly supportive of me doing all these swims,
..un more than I ever could have expected. Me taking time
away from our family and from her. I've tried to minimize the
impact on everyone by swimming early in the morning, but that
also has meant that I go to bed at 8 or 9pm. I really appreciate
being so happily married to such a great, successful woman.

As I was getting stuff ready and for most of the car ride, I
thought about the many failures and most challenging points in
my life. The split. Wild Sparks. Catalina. Losing 40% of the
company and our biggest client. Not continuing swimming at
Cal after my freshman year. Not finishing my graduate degree.
Law School. Juan de Fuca. I thought about what I had learned
from each and how they made me stronger. How they'd tested
me. I kept thinking, "What doesn't kill me, makes me stronger."
The phrase "This too shall pass" kept playing in my head as
something I'd need out there. I'd say these phrases in my head
many times during the swim and I knew I'd be wondering if I
had what it would take. I also wondered if I'd be lucky.

I understood at this point, like never before, that I learn at least
as much from my failures as I do from my successes. What is
hardest makes me stronger. The most trying personal trials are
what make me who I am and give me strength when I need it.

I never would have guessed that I'd be thinking about failures on
my way to the boat to swim the Irish Sea, or that it would be a
good thing.

Greasing Up

There was no wind when we got to the pier at Donaghadee a
little before 6am. Quinton had move the jump time 30 minutes

later to account for what he'd seen on Saturday, but by the time I'd heard from him, it was too late to tell anyone...I sent an email, to take some of the pressure off, but I kept the crew meeting time the same. We were the first there (Sarah right behind us). Owen came next a little before 6am (he was coming from Dublin) followed by Brian right at 6am, and Quinton at about 6:30am. It was relatively warm (probably 65F/18C). There was no wind, but it seemed a little muggy. The best weather we could hope for on the Irish side.

Quinton's crew started showing up around 7am and the observer (Gary) showed up right at 7:30am. We left the pier at 7:30am. Sue gave me a huge hug as did each of the kids. She was confident, but also a little worried, since she wouldn't be out there with me. She'd really wanted to be on the boat, but I didn't want here there. I knew it might be really bad, and I also know how much she loves me. I didn't want to be thinking about her worrying on the boat.

We motored over to the jump point (a few hundred yards away—the closest point to Scotland). Sarah started putting the grease on. She used just about all of it. I'd prefer to go without, but the grease is highly important for jellyfish and chafing. The jellyfish tend to slide off faster, lessening the effects. Also, I'd grown out my beard. It was more than two inches long now. With my cap, goggles, and beard, my face would be mostly protected. I wore the grease most of the way down my arms, and to my ankles. Cam had also given me some jellyfish sting neutralizing lotion, which he said helped. It was mixed in the grease, along with Lanolin, Vaseline, and zinc oxide (Desatin).

Cold Water

The water was flat when I started. Like every other swim, it was cold when I dove in. I touched the rock, put up my arm and started.

I breathed every four then every two. That pattern and the whooshing sounds of my arms entering and going by below me would be the vast majority of everything I would hear over the next 12 hours, if I was lucky.

I started seeing lots of jellyfish. Moon jellies are small and white, about 6-18 (15-45cm) inches wide—they don't sting much at all. Compass are about 18-36 inches (a half to one meter) wide, with 3-6 foot (1-2m) tentacles—they sting but not as bad as the lion's manes and are more translucent.

I was also seeing (and managing to avoid swimming into) a couple dozen lion's manes. These are mostly 18-36 inches (.5m-1m) wide, darker centers with fine hair-like tentacles stretching 9-12 feet (3-4m).

These were all below the surface, mostly about 1.5-3 feet (a half to one meter) down. This meant I could see them, stop suddenly, and go around them or use a shallow stroke if one surprised me. The jellyfish in this part lasted until about 3.5 hours in. I lost a fair amount of time going around them, but it was better than getting stung a lot. I did feel about a half dozen stings, but none bad. I suspect that the neutralizer was doing its job, as well as the grease. I also knew I hadn't hit any straight on.

I swam fast the first 4 hours, fast and comfortable. The feeds were lasting 30-40 seconds. I was feeling good. At one hour, and every half hour until 4 hours, I fed on one packet of Gu chews (good, delicious, I had them in my suit!) and warm water or 50/50 warm water and Snapple. I was taking in about 8 oz per feed. Everything was going well. I was past Phia, who had left about 30 minutes before us, and Keith was still behind me. He had started about 30 minutes behind me. I was pretty sure he'd be a little faster (maybe 30 minutes?) if we both made it, and nothing else was different. My position relative to Keith was a good indication that I was doing well.

Dizzy, Hallucinating

At about 4 hours, I took a whole bottle (14 oz) of warm water with a little tea. I'd asked the crew to crush acetaminophen (Tylenol), naproxen sodium (Aleve), and a couple of Zyrtec. There wasn't another good way to get them to me. What came next was not good. I couldn't eat or drink and the Tylenol and water was sloshing around in my stomach. I had far too much liquid (2x what I should have had), and the tea and Tylenol had made my stomach sour. I started burping up, and suddenly not getting any glucose to my brain.

The next 3 hours were a blur. I was dizzy, disoriented, hallucinating. I imagined there were big concrete piers (like telephone poles in the water) in front of me, even though I couldn't see in front of me (I was breathing to the left side). I had to look up every so often just to make sure I wasn't going crazy. I thought there was a pier (dock) on the right side of me. I breathe to my left, so I was just seeing the boat on the left and no even looking right.

The boat was blurry, and it was at the same time, both way too bright, and way too dark.

I've been here before. Catalina. What doesn't kill me....

I knew what to do. I couldn't get cold like I did in Catalina...the water was too cold here. First thing, stroke rate. I realized my stroke rate had fallen below 60. It hadn't been there long, I was still warm inside, although really cold outside. My arms hurt. My shoulders hurt. My back hurt. Ok, my stroke rate was back up. Now I needed to assess.

Core is good still. Arms—ok, my right hand is numb, especially my thumb and forefinger. Let's stretch them out. Probably something about the way I'm landing my right hand at the front of my stroke—clean up my stroke—can't just be faster, has to be clean, too. Forget about pulling a lot of water for now, let's just see if we can fix my right wrist/hand. Ok, stretching it out feels a little better, but that's as much as I'm going to get. I'll be swimming with it numb the rest of the swim. I can do that.

Concentrate...think about the entry. What can I feel? I can feel my pinky. I can feel my elbow. Not much between. Left hand is better, not feeling much but can still feel the water—at least not numb. Ok, right elbow, need to get feedback from you. How is my right hand landing? Eyes, look. I'm going in pinky first. Brian is swimming on the boat. No, he's trying to tell me to stretch out on my right side. He's a good swimmer and he could see what was wrong and tell me how to fix it without words.

Ok, stroke is better for now but I'll have to keep thinking about it. Let's try not to burp. Ok, coming up on 4.5 hours. How do I feed? Let's try Stinger gummies—more calories. Wow, that didn't work. Better spitting them up then puking them up, though. Back in the basket. No way I'm drinking anything—I learned something in Catalina, to fix too much liquid, don't drink for a while. It is a risk, but it worked last time. 15 second stop, and I'm done. If they said anything, I didn't hear it. I know

Sarah wanted me to drink. She looks worried. No way I was going to drink. Not next time either.

Concentrate. Try not to burp up. Either throw up, or keep it all in. I don't throw up. Only one choice left: keep it in.

I can swim for another few more hours, but I'm not even half way done yet. I'm not going to finish.

That was the last time I thought that. I started thinking about Catalina. I thought,

Just get through this. I didn't think I'd finish Catalina, but I just kept going. What doesn't kill you makes you stronger. This too shall pass.

At the last feed, Gary (observer) had said, "Concentrate on someone you hate." I didn't hear him say, "...and imagine killing them." That would have made me laugh and would have given me quite a bit to think about. Instead, having only heard the first part, I thought,

I don't hate anyone (at least I couldn't think of anyone). But Attila—he was a bit arrogant. I have to get through this. I have to show him how it is done. Attila isn't a bad guy, but he's going to help me here—I hope he doesn't hate me for using him to focus.

What's up with the right wrist? Okay, not good. Stretch. That hurt...at least I felt something. That tendon or muscle between my wrist and thumb...stretch it again. Yep, that's it. It's wasted. Can I still use it? Yes, just know it is hurt, much more than the rest of my arms.

Ok, continue with the assessment. They're all blurry on deck and it is too bright, but I can see underwater. This

isn't Copenhagen. This is a glucose thing, not cold thing. I can just sight on the boat from underwater. First problem solved. I'll mostly close my eyes when I breathe. No need to look above water for now. If I start hallucinating hot women in bikinis on the boat, I'll start looking above water, but for now, just watch the bottom of the boat and concentrate on stroke count.

Pec muscles are hurting. Ok, much more than other swims, but just muscle, I can handle that and a lot more. Upper back: traps are better than usual for coming up on five hours. Pecs hurt...any idea why? No.

Okay, 5 mins to the 5-hour feed. Use left hand to get feed...wait, I'm not stopping. Yell, "No feed." Sarah is clearly not happy. That's her job, but I know I'm right. She can't make me drink if I keep swimming.

Blocking out the cement pilings and the long pier to my right. Not tempted to look there anymore. They are not real. Let them stay there...if I run into them, I'll know I was mistaken. A Beautiful Mind. *They don't exist.*

What is the Buddhist saying, "acknowledge your thoughts then let them go," or something like that. Ok, brain, feel free to tell me whatever you want. I'm only believing what I'm pretty sure is true. I'm cold on the outside, but my core is rising in temperature. It is probably at least 95 right now.

They're telling me five minutes to next feed. I yell again, "No feed." Ok, I think I'm at 5.5 hours. Everything is still blurry, but Brian just wrote stroke rate is 68. That is good. It's what it was when I started. I'm usually slower (more efficient) in the Bay, but this is longer than the 5-hour and 7.5-hour swims that I did with the Locos and Dusty in Jan and Feb. Those were cold, but...I did those. I'm not at 7.5 hours yet. I can come back from this. "Just keep swimming" (like Dory in Finding Nemo*).*

They give me the 5-minute signal again. I agree, but I don't eat or drink. I tell them try again in 15 minutes. It is now 6 hours. After about 15 seconds, I continue.

Sprained Wrist

It was still cold.

I'm feeling a little better. My stomach has now settled a bit. My stroke rate is good...I think about 68. My right wrist still hurts, not just a little. My thumb and forefinger are still numb, but the numbness hasn't spread. My stroke is cleaner, but Brian is still telling me to stretch my stroke out. As I come up on 6 hours and 15 minutes, I tell them 15 more minutes. I'm doing better, but they don't know it yet. I'm not out of the woods. A drink could send me back to a bad place.

It is still blurry, but not as bad, not as bright, and not dark anymore. The hallucinations are under control...still there, but I know they are not real. I had the same pier in Catalina (the pilings are new, though). I guess these are just a function of swimming when it gets really hard. I know what to do next time—hope for bikinis instead of concrete.

At 6 hours and 30 minutes into the swim, I took a feed. The crew is worried about me not feeding. I take a small sip of water, not more than 2 oz. (50ml). There'll be no more tea for sure. I take a Gu (90 calories, no caffeine). It tastes good. Back to swimming.

Coming up on 7 hours, I started to feel like I could pull water again, more than just keeping my stroke count high. I put a little effort into it. I was back. I was sure the crew saw it, too.

At 7 hours, I had water (about 5 oz, 125ml) and a Gu chews. They tasted good. I was through a pretty rough patch. Now it was time to start making up some time.

> *Assessment: core warm, skin cold. Right hand functional. Just need to concentrate on putting it in the right place. Good form. Rest of my body fine, better than expected after 7+ hours. All about staying loose and pulling a lot of water. Need to keep that right hand doing its job. Need to feel without having any feeling in my hands. Riding higher in the water. Good. Stroke is better. Rate is good.*

I pushed each of the next two feeds to 45 minutes. Each was one gel and 4 oz./100ml warm water. I was moving well.

Time and Mind Games

As we approached the next feed, I remember thinking, at my next feed I'd be at 9 hours. About that time, Brian wrote "4 MORE HOURS" (which would have meant 13 hours total). About 5 minutes later, he changed it to "3 MORE HOURS."

Either he got it wrong the first time, or something changed (or maybe both). In any case, he wouldn't have written the 3 more hours unless Quinton told him too.

I decided it was safest to assume that it was still 4 more hours. I could do that. It was time to start planning on the last 6 feeds. Heads down water polo stroke...nice and limber, fast, on top of the water.

I was moving reasonably fast at that point. I had tried not to look at Scotland, but I could no longer see Ireland at all anymore. I took a quick peak. Scotland was there. I tried not to look, though. Big features appear way closer than they are. I didn't want to lull myself into thinking I was closer than I was. Also, looking forward it hard on your neck on a long swim. Four more hours (I'd consciously not subtracted time I'd swum since Brian had written 4 then 3 hours, and I'd even discounted the message as well. I was now assuming at least 4 more hours even though I knew it was likely far less.

Then I moved it to 5 hours to be conservative. A round trip Baker Beach is a little over 5 hours. I thought, "I'm taking off from the club right now. I'll be back soon." Feeds varied between 30 and 45 minutes. I'd lost track of how far I was across. I knew I only had 4 or 5 hours left in my head. I also knew that 5 hours was a lie, but I was getting myself mentally prepared for the worst possible case.

> *I've got this. I'm going to finish. I'm hoping Brian will tell me how far we'd come in miles on the white board so I could figure out my overall pace and maybe compare my 30-minute progress to my overall pace to see if I'm going faster. I'm doing well now. Time to get there. I'm going to make this for sure. Only 5 hours left.*

A little while later, I realized there were good things that happened within 4 hours of finishing (and I was maybe closer to 2 hours out, but I wasn't going to think that). At 5 minutes before the feed, I asked for one of the two cinnamon buns I'd packed. Actually, I don't really remember asking for it, but somehow they got it for me. I think they had ESP. I was only able to get 2/3 of it down with some warm water. My next thoughts were:

That was my longest feed by far, probably well over a minute, but it tasted a dream and was worth swimming for. That was the first bready, sweet thing I'd had in almost six years.

I'm going to keep swimming so I can get the other 1/3. Six years since my last cinnamon bun...wow, good. I have to do more swims so I can continue to get this kind of carbs every once in a while. That was yummy.

After the feed, I equated what was left to a RT GG (from the club to the Golden Gate Bridge and back). That is 9 miles and change, a little over 4 hours, but maybe more if the tides were not good. I knew I was probably a lot closer, but that was ok. I wanted to be ready for the worst. I'd done RT GG so many times. It wasn't easy, but it was easily within my wheelhouse, even right now. I tried to imagine swimming in the Bay, but it was too distracting. Instead, I decided to concentrate on my stroke and staying on top of the water. Loping water polo stroke...loose and powerful.

At my next feed, they gave me half of the second cinnamon roll. It was good, but maybe a little much. I only ate 2/3 of what they gave me. It was still delicious. They told me I was now four miles out.

Quickly doing the math, I realize we're probably within 2 hours, and a voice I'm trying to ignore says that it is much less at this faster pace. It is 3 hours or less now, but I can't pretend that it is still 4 hours anymore.

I still wasn't completely sure that I'd made it through the current that typically washes swimmers away from Scotland. To make it through, you need a hard push near the end. I wanted to ask if we were through it, but I didn't dare stop. I decided, "If I've got 2-3 hours left, I can go hard for at least that long. I'll break through at some point." I picked it up. I started pushing a lot of water, finishing every stroke, especially on my left side, but even now on my right, too. I stretched a couple of times, quickly, but didn't lose any time in doing so.

I had been peeing in the first four hours, but that stopped during the dark time. I couldn't then no matter how hard I tried. I even tried stopping all together (usually I can pee while swimming by just easing off my kick). At about this time, I started peeing regularly again. I didn't know it, but I was well past 9.5 hours at that point. I was motoring now. I was pretty sure they could see it from the boat. I was going to finish for sure.

Pain and Swearing

At about 10 hours, roughly 3 miles from shore, I started seeing a ton of lion's mane jellyfish. I remember thinking, "How could I say I'd swum the Irish Sea if I'd barely been stung?" I'd figured at least I had the six at the beginning. I'd take a day like today...it is about finishing. I needed to tip-toe through these.

They were big. Jello-like with dark brown centers, many as wide as a cooktop. Tentacles stretched to twice my height, all tangled and floating on the surface. I stopped and went around a lot of them and saw even more just outside or just beneath my hands. I had counted roughly a hundred pretty quickly. These lion's manes were far more poisonous than the moons and compass jellies I'd encountered earlier.

The first one I hit bounced off my face. It quickly enveloped me, covering me from face to feet. I screamed loud. It was on the surface, tentacles floating. I didn't see it until the head was bouncing off me down my right side. The head had bounced off my face first (beard worked). I didn't get stung as much on my face, but my neck down was electric and burning. It was like being stung by lots of bees, having people burn you with cigarette butts, and getting 15 Amps of 110V all at once. It was worse than the worst shock I'd ever had, and it lasted a lot longer, too. I untangled myself like it was seaweed. I was swearing. Not crying, swearing.

About 2 or 3 minutes later, I started to gain some control over the pain. Then the second one hit me. This seemed to get any spots that had been missed by the first. It stung me through my suit (yes, even there). It hit my torso pretty hard, more legs and feet than arms. I caught a clue and started looking more carefully for them as soon as I was untangled.

I went around a bunch of them over the next few minutes, but another one surprised me. This third one was the most worst, and hurt the most on impact. It might have been just that I already had some toxin in me, but it was bad. I was less tangled with it, but damn, it hurt. I didn't scream or swear at all. I just needed to get through it.

I was ready for the next one, hurting but ready. I knew I only had about an hour left. Fuckin' jellyfish weren't going to stop me now.

That next jellyfish never came. I saw more, but after about 10 minutes they started disappearing. I swam harder. My adrenaline was up, and it was time to finish. The stings distracted me from how much my arms and shoulders hurt, so I just pushed it back up to the speed I was going before the jellyfish. The stings hurt a lot, but I just pushed the pain out of my mind. I think I had one more feed about 15 minutes later, but I don't remember it well. Quinton was getting worried about me finishing before the tide turned. Owen and Gary communicated this to me. It was now slack, but wouldn't be for long.

At the next feed, Brian told me that he could see individual rocks. About 30 minutes after that, I was able to, too. A few minutes later, the boat stopped. I was probably 200 yards/meters from the rocks. I swam some heads-up free and chose my landing spot. Then I started looking at the bottom.

I was in Scotland. I was about to finish. It was pretty clear, and individual rocks were coming up closer to the surface. I got to about 25 or 30 yards/meters out, and I started to swim breast stroke in the shallow, rocky water. I was now swimming very slowly. Breast was far harder for me than free at this point. I sculled face down and watched the rocks as I started washing into shore with the waves. The shore was all rocks just above the water's surface, at the base of the cliffs. I chose my rock, a relatively flat one that came gradually out of the water. I put a hand on the top out of the water, and raised my hand up as I was instructed to at the beginning. I didn't waste any time. I turned around and did 3 strokes of breast, then I started swimming the 200 yards/meters back to the boat freestyle. It was easy swimming out to the boat, but I knew I couldn't linger or I'd get cold.

Back on the Boat

I looked back at Scotland as I was getting on the boat, trying to savor the moment and remember the view. The sun had already gone down. My eyes took in what they could.

I got onto the boat easily. I was still strong. I think I could have swum another 2-4 more hours. I'd prepared for 14-16 hours. Although I'm not so sure I could have done 16, I think I could have made 14. Gary said that had I gone on Saturday, I would have made it. At that point, I wasn't sure, but reflecting upon it, I think I could have. The thing is that every day in any channel (even the same day) is different and presents different challenges. Saturday might not have been my day. One thing I knew though, Sunday was my day. I'd done it.

It felt good: 11 hours and 19 minutes. It had been mostly 54 degrees (12C). I did it.

I had the other half of the cinnamon roll, and some water. Brian gave me four rashers of bacon. Irish bacon is thin-cut smoked pork chops—best bacon anywhere. Oh, man, did it taste good.

Owen cleaned the grease off me with the two disposable towels I'd bought. Just for that one act (if not for all the cheering and for the advice to Sarah and Brian during the swim), he'll always have my eternal gratitude. That grease is the grossest stuff anywhere. While he was cleaning me off, Sarah called Sue and handed me the phone. The call didn't last long. The reception was ok, but I was down inside the boat where it was warmer and noisier.

I had some more food (nuts, I think) and more water. Probably other food, too, but not a lot. I talked to people a little. Then, once I was dressed I laid down on a bench and took a nap. It was time to sleep, and it didn't matter much where I was. I was asleep the instant my head came to rest on the bench. I slept for about 90 minutes. When I woke up, we were about 30 minutes from Donaghadee.

I talked to everyone for the rest of the ride in, then Sarah saw the kids climbing on the Pier and pointed them out to me. I started waving and immediately picked Sue out of the crowd. She was waving hardest of all.

It took about 30 minutes to get our stuff off the boat. Shubham was coming down to meet us (what a great guy, I'm sure he was exhausted), but we needed to get me home at that point. Also, I hadn't taken or put on any meds yet, and the stings were starting to burn and hurt a lot more as I was getting warmed up.

The cold (what gets most people) didn't have much of an impact (my extra 15 lbs./7 kg. really helped), but the distance wore down my arms and shoulders. At the end of the day, the jellyfish didn't have any impact on my swim. Although I was worried about the jellies, if anything they made the last part of the swim faster, if even only for an hour.

Lion's Mane Jellyfish

16 – Those Who Finished and Didn't

As I sat at 7am on Monday morning, wiped-out and burning up
with jellyfish stings, I jotted down a few thoughts. A few weeks
later, I came back and rounded the thoughts out.

Analysis

I was the 6th this year, the 33rd person to accomplish it overall, and the 11th fastest as of September 2016. One more person finished (Phia, #34 for the year). It appears unlikely that anyone else will finish this year.

Shubham and Attila did not finish on Saturday. Three of us finished on Sunday (Keith, me, and Phia, in that order). Xarris didn't finish despite a strong attempt. That is 3 of 6 in one weekend—more attempts and more successes than any window before. I think one more person might have finished a week later.

I got some insight into Shubham's swim on the way back. He was pulled out unconscious after 12 hours in the water, a little less than 6 miles from Scotland. Shubham is an incredible person and athlete. Expect great things from him.

The early wind tired him out. When he got to the current off Scotland where he needed that extra push, he had nothing left and the cold got him. He was in almost an hour longer than me. There is no shame in that attempt. He waited for another month, but the weather did not cooperate. He went back to India without making it across.

Also on Saturday, Attila was pulled out after 8 hours, also unconscious. He was still far from Scotland. He was in worse shape and having a seizure, and was med-evac'ed to the hospital. I saw him a couple of days later. He recovered quickly.

He was not ready for the cold. He'd put in a handful of weeks of training in the cold water, but even for a record-setting ultra-marathon swimmer, a lot of cold-water training is critical to making a 54F/12C ultra-marathon swim. I also think that mentally he was not ready. He wanted to "break the record."

The goal is just to finish. Sometimes luck can be coupled with one's ability to make it across, but often even finishing is out of one's control. I hope he takes a year and tries again, with more cold-water training behind him.

Keith set the men's record at a little less than 10 hours. No one can take a finish away, and it'll take a very strong, fast, acclimatized swimmer on a very good day with very good luck and a great pilot to beat Keith's time, although I'm sure it will happen eventually.

Phia finished, surprising me and many others. Her time was over 14 hours. I have a great deal of respect for her. It is hard to be in cold water for 14 hours.

Attila and Shubham were very lucky. About two weeks after we were in the North Channel, an experienced ultra-marathon swimmer died attempting the English Channel. Although the water was 9F (5C) warmer, 63F/17C is still cold. Sixteen hours in, his body temperature, already low, fell further, and he just stopped swimming. His crew tried everything, but he died of heart failure resulting from hypothermia. He was 1 mile from France. There is real risk in this sport.

Is the Irish Sea Getting Easier?

More people have done the Irish Sea this year than ever before, which begs the question, "Why?"

Someone posited that the Irish Sea is getting warmer or has fewer jellies. I'd say no to both, based on my experience.

It was about 54F/12C. This was about 5F/2.5C below my EC swim 20 years ago, which is what I'd always heard it was in August. I don't think the North Channel is any warmer now than it was 20 years ago.

Likewise, I saw about 700 jellyfish (400 moon, 200 compass, and by far the worst, the 100 lion's mane near the end on the surface). I got stung about a half dozen times early in the swim, but the jellyfish lotion seemed to have minimized the impact of those. I still felt them but they weren't bad. I don't know which type they were (I hadn't seen them), but they were probably compass or broken off tentacles from lion's manes.

The cream comes off, though, and it doesn't help later in the swim when they seem worst. I got hit more than Cam, Andrew, Keith, or Phia, from what they described, but none of us had it as bad as Kim. That is a very small sample. I spent a lot of time swimming around jellyfish through about 4 hours of the swim. I probably spent as much time swimming around jellies as I spent feeding. Each likely accounted for about 15 minutes. I think jellies are just part of the North Channel, and I don't think they are less than they were before.

I'm not sure how other people count, but if I count each tentacle that burned me, I probably took about 40 lashes—not nearly what Kim experienced. Kim said she had "around 100 stings." I think these are comparative numbers. My skin was on fire for two days, even with meds. Like 40 bee stings. Then they turned into 400 bumps, each like one mosquito bite—400 mosquito bites.

I think everyone gets stung, it is just a matter of luck as to how bad, when, and how many times. While it was painful and hard, it didn't make my time any slower. I was prepared mentally for it and it didn't affect me.

The three of us (Keith, Phia, and I) had perfect wind and current conditions, as did Cameron and Andrew McLaughlin. WindGuru and other apps have made choosing good days more likely. There are very few good days on the North Channel, as demonstrated by Shubham's bad luck with weather.

What Does It Take to Make It Across?

What is it that the Irish Sea requires? Here's the list (just my opinion):

- swimming strength (the ability to have and tap reserves late in a swim)
- mental attitude and focus
- cold water acclimatization
- body fat (not skinny)
- swimming speed
- good conditions (wind especially, also tide and current)
- good piloting
- good crew
- good luck

I trained at SERC, but also found colder places. I swam through the winter in the Bay (49 this year). In spring, I swam in Tahoe, Chicago, Ireland, Copenhagen, and Santa Cruz, in addition to the attempt of Juan de Fuca. SERC alone would not have been enough for me. I needed colder water to acclimatize, but the SF Bay provides a great base to train in, both from a swimming perspective and from a support perspective.

I also didn't do any pool training (Cam didn't either, although Keith did quite a bit). I think speed, cold, and the ability to focus, along with long colder swims are the keys. All of us had those. Also, although Kim and Phia aren't as fast, they both seem to make up for it with focus and determination, and a good amount of acclimatization. I'm finding, that like feeding, there is no single recipe that is right, and on one day one recipe might be better than another. Being mentally and physically prepared for the challenge and being ready for the possibility of failure is absolutely key.

As I'm getting older, I've had to balance training with recovery. My plan was far different than Keith's (about 8 years younger), Cam's (about 15 years younger), or Shubham's (almost 30 years younger). Shubham had did everything right that was within his control, and still didn't make it (didn't even get a chance to go in September). All four of us each got in a lot of training miles (probably about the same on average) in cold water, but we each focused differently on what was most effective for us. None of us trained in warm water, then tried to acclimatize quickly. All of us have some speed, and all of us did a lot of long swims in cold water in the last 6 months.

On the North Channel success rate: I remember the figure 8% success from 20 years ago (that may have been anecdotal). I'd guess it is closer to 20% historically, now, given the success rates the last few years. This season, the success rate is just over 50% with about a dozen attempts. With more focus on it (more ultra-marathon swimmers doing it and having done it), training methods getting better, we learn from both successes and failures. Also, with better tools (WindGuru, especially) the pilots are choosing better days. The number of successes is still relatively low. It will never be like Catalina or the English Channel, but the rate and numbers are indeed climbing. I don't think the swim is any less tough, but more people are better prepared and those few, precious good weather days are easier to predict, meaning fewer failures and more successes.

What Is Next For Me?

I hope to do more similarly outrageous swims. My cherry-on-top of the Oceans7 will probably be something no one has ever done, shorter and colder in Scandinavia (to play to my strengths). Hopefully, it will be something very much out of reach for most cold-water ultra-marathon swimmers. I also still plan to finish the Oceans7 and go back and complete Juan de Fuca. First, though, I'm going to take 2 months mostly off before I really start training again.

After the Swim

First thing Monday morning, Sue brought me and the kids to get me a shave and a haircut in Belfast. The beard had served its purpose and kept my face protected from the jellyfish. But I hated it. It tasted like whatever I had eaten last, and it itched like crazy. I was very happy to have it gone. I looked like a Yedi.

Sue the girls went home for water polo and work the next day. The tickets for Ethan and me were still 5 days out, and changing them would have cost more than the original RT tickets had cost. So we took a few days to travel to London (figured out a work reason to be there), and then we went back to Dublin.

It worked out nicely that I was able to put Shubham into our very nice place for a few nights, and I was also able to leave him all of my feeds, plus the food in the fridge. I probably could have checked out a few days early without having to pay for the room, and the feeds would have been good for me in my upcoming swims, but I can always buy more. These things just seemed like the right things to do. Shubham was on a tight budget, and he's a person who deserves to have good things happen to him. It was my first chance to pay it forward for what Keith, Sarah, Oonagh, and Brian had done for me. I only wish he'd gotten the chance to swim.

Padraig and Jacqueline were also such incredibly positive influences, offering advice, making our trip fun, and helping Shubham. They are great ambassadors for our sport, and represent the very best that is what I love about this sport.

I can't ever match Ruth's generosity (cancelling her vacation to help Shubham, and putting him up at her house afterwards), nor will I ever be able to repay Sarah, Keith, Oonagh, or Brian, or ever even come close. Their support and their energy was amazing. Sarah works on a suicide prevention line and this has been a tough year for her. Yet she still devoted a huge amount of time and energy to helping me. Brian took time away from his life and his family to help me, even not drinking at his niece's wedding and driving through the night (both before and after the swim). He never for a moment showed me how tired he must have been.

Likewise, Owen and Gary weren't out there for themselves that day. They were out there for me, and the jacket I got for Owen and the very small amount that Gary got as a stipend, don't come close to comparing to what they gave to me on this day. Even Quinton, whom I paid well to guide me across, is someone I owe a debt to. He was always positive, helpful, and he got me there. He has done a great job combining his work, leisure, helping people, and even family (his son is his partner in the marina). He's successful in my mind.

I've learned a lot from all of these people. I have a lot of paying-it-back and a lot of paying-it-forward to do.

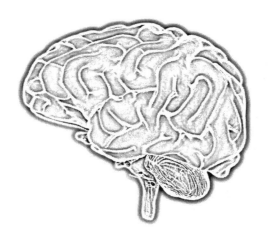

17 – The Last Word

Why would I ever combine swimming and business in a book? What do they have in common, and how do either relate to the wider world around us, or to any one person besides me?

I might have written this just because business and swimming are the two things that I'm most interested in, and I like to pontificate (even if I'm just pretending that people will read it).

While I'm sure that's true to some degree, I put these two topics together for three reasons.

Ben Franklin

I think that each has lessons that can be valuable to the other and to everyone. These include:

1. Luck favors the prepared. (Stolen from Edna in my favorite movie, *The Incredibles*).
2. No matter how much you prepare, luck will have a hand in everything you do.
3. Hard work pays off. Smart hard work pays off even more.
4. Know your own strengths and weaknesses.
5. Get back up when you fall down. Every failure is part of ultimate success.

All Boy Scout, Ben Franklin stuff I admit, but all true, too.

Tell a Good Story Well

I wanted to provide some interesting stories. The stories illustrate a key point—that both ultimate success and smaller successes come from taking lots of outrageous risks and failing a lot. That is the theme of the book. I hope it is a good read.

Most Important

If you've been paying attention, this last one won't have snuck up on you. The real reason I wrote this book was to illustrate a bigger, more important point. I'll explain.

If you think about it, you want to be judged on your whole body of your work. One small failure or even large success does not define any of us. That means that no matter who you are or what you believe in, your reckoning will come late in your life, likely as you approach your last breath. We feel so bad when someone dies young because they didn't get a chance to fulfill their dreams, to be successful, by whatever standard they chose.

For those of us who are leading full lives, we want to be able to look forward to a day when we can honestly say, "My life has been a success." Likewise, you want to be able to look back over your life and relive the things that got you there. Daniel Kahneman discussed this at the very end of an excellent (but thick) book called, *Thinking Fast and Thinking Slow*.

Success is defined by each of us. The first thing each of us needs to do is to decide what success means. Big picture, end of life success. Who do we want to have been?

Once we're there, we need to ask a lot of questions. What is important? What things need to be done? What are the goals? Will this path get us there? What should be included? What experiences do we want to have along the way?

The path should include outrageous risks and the potential to fail, because we learn from failure. It should include a lot of success, too, because success gives us strength and confidence, and earns us respect from others. Success also provides us with opportunities to do more.

We should choose goals that are ridiculous.

Do cool stuff. No outrageous or outlandish idea is too big to try. Take risks, and don't be scared by failure. Failure is something to always be prepared for. Don't worry too much about how you'll look if you fail. Don't try to fail, in fact try hard not to, but don't be afraid to fail often and learn a lot each time.

Success isn't determined at the end of the day or at the end of our lives by how many goals we reached, by how much money we made, by our record of swims, or conversely by how many times we failed.

It is determined by who we are. By what we do for those around us. By how we contributed to our communities and the world.

The best people I know are those who are always there for others. People I have the most respect for always think of how they can help and what they can give. Each of these incredible people has their own unique way of helping, of giving. Each of these people fit my definition of success.

Also, almost to a person, these people are mentors in some capacity—as parents, teachers, coaches, managers, leaders, or just sharing with those who can use the help.

Money is good. It can be one of many tools to help you help others. Experiences are great, too. They can help you be a better mentor. Experience can buy you credibility that might help you help others. Neither, though, are ultimate success. It is what you do with them. It is all about helping people, giving back. Do things that help you be in a position that you can give back, but ultimately, give back, much more than you get.

Think about scale. Do it big. Apply those same outrageous goals to giving.

Help create the ideal world that you want to live in. Even if you don't have money. There are 168 hours in a week. We work 40 of those hours, and sleep another 50 or so. That leaves almost 80 hours to eat, drink, have fun, work toward our ultimate goals, and drive toward our ultimate success. Just by filling the in-between time differently, you can accomplish a lot more.

If you do it right, you can find confluence between work, leisure, family, and big goals and working toward success. If you can this to scale, wow.

The more you do, the more confluence you will find. The universe has a way of causing good things to be possible. This all involves change and flexibility, which is hard for most people. Take a chance. Make the changes you need to be ultimately successful, and figure out ways to help other people—big or small.

Set lofty goals. Do things that are crazy hard, that most people say are impossible. Make them possible. Think about your ultimate goal, or that moment before everything proverbially flashes before your eyes. What do you want to see? Now is the time to start making those things happen.

In the short term, remember that success will give you opportunities to help people. Ultimately, remember that success is not about the little personal successes, but it is how much you are able to help others.

Appendix A – Feeding

Catalina was a real wake-up call. I was going to need to figure out how to feed. Out of the water, I had it pretty dialed in, even if I had had a bit more carbs in the past month than I should have.

When you are swimming in cold-water, if your blood glucose level drops, you get cold. Even most well trained marathon swimmers can't recover from a significant drop in core temperature caused by low blood sugar. What's more, there are only three outcomes when core temperature drops due to low blood sugar: 1) you get out, 2) you manage to increase your blood glucose level before your temperature drops too far (from burning body fat or from taking on carbs or less efficiently, protein), 3) you die.

That sounds really melodramatic—you die? There are lots of risks in this sport (boats, jellyfish, the one-in-a-million chance of getting bitten by a shark), but really every open-water swimmer knows that the real risk is hypothermia.

This sport has has real danger to it, even to well-trained open-water swimmers, especially as the water gets colder. The coast guard has a rule called the 50-50-50 rule. For an untrained person, after 50 minutes in 50F water, there is a 50% survival rate. For a trained swimmer, this rule doesn't apply (we are good at shunting blood away from our skin), but if blood glucose levels fall, stroke rate drops. If Stroke rate drops, heart rate drops. Energy output drops. If energy output drops, heat production drops. When heat production drops, core temperature drops.

It is normal to see core body temperature a couple of degrees (to about 96-97F, or 36C) just being in cold-water. Well-trained cold-water swimmers can get down to 94-95F (35C)—they'd be cold ("bone cold") but a good sauna and will warm them up in 10-30 minutes. Good cold-water swimmers can even bring their temperature back up from lower temperatures (92-93F or 34C) by swimming harder. But you can't swim harder if your blood glucose level is low.

The hardest part of swimming is understanding the difference between merely being cold (which you always are in cold water), and knowing you cannot warm up. If you're blood-glucose level has dropped and your core temperature has likewise fallen below 94F (about 35C), the chances that most swimmers will warm up are not so good.

With low blood glucose (and the resultant lower heat output), core temperature can drop to a dangerous level (90-91F/33F or below) in a matter of 5-10 minutes or less. This is when you start feeling sleepy. With little glucose, your brain starts to get very cloudy. Vision gets blurred. Thoughts are very slow, and concentration is non-existent. Muscle movement becomes lethargic. Feeding (glucose levels) and body temperature are very tightly related, even in 70F (21C) water.

Oddly, many swimmers keep swimming, their arms still moving (an automatic thing for swimmers) when they are hypothermic. The last thing a crew observes before death is that a swimmer stops breathing, even though their arms are still going. I know of instances where friends were crewing and they had to pull swimmers like this. In both cases, they were watching their swimmers near the end of channel swims. The swimmers were cold (and like most channel swimmers, not saying anything about it). In both cases, the swimmers just kept swimming, 20, 30, 40 strokes without a breath, before someone jumped in to "wake them up." In both cases, the swim was instantly ended (if a swimmer is touched and it is not incidental, the swimmer is disqualified). The swimmers were upset, but both would have died had they not been turned over and pulled out, as their core temperatures had fallen down to 90F or below.

Generally, most ultra-marathon cold-water swimmers end their swims with body temperatures between 94-96F (35-36C). Below a core of 94F (35C), if blood glucose level is low, it is unlikely that core temperature will rise without external heat, and it just becomes a matter of time before the swim is over. Some swimmers can come back from temperatures of 91-93F (33.5-34.5C), but it is very hard to do for even the very best conditioned and acclimatized cold-water ultra-marathon swimmers, and it won't happen if blood-glucose levels are low or the swimmer is at a point of exhaustion.

Swimming burns a lot of calories. Also, keeping warm means generating heat internally. With a consistent heart rate of about 110-120 bpm (required to stay warm), you'll likely be burning 800-1200 calories per hour. The current consensus is that we can only sustainably take in about 450-550 calories per hour (less for many people, more for some). That leaves a shortfall of 250-750 calories per hour.

Now, the good news is that you have plenty of fat (no, I'm not looking at you, or judging you—I'm assuming you look like me, and no one has ever called me skinny.

Our bodies have at least tens of thousands of calories. Most people feel that a pound of fat has about 3,500 calories (or if you burn 3,500 calories that you don't replace, you'll lose a pound of fat). This is a very rough estimate, and it doesn't exactly correlate to the real world, but I've noticed that on bigger swims (say, 20k and over) I lose about 2-6 lbs. after I've rehydrated. Most of that is fat but a small part of that is also catabolized muscle. I tend to rebalance very quickly. Unfortunately, the pounds don't stay off.

The big problem with burning fat, is that you have to be both in desperate need (like a bear is chasing you, and you've already used up your more immediate sugar stores), and you have to have enough sugar in your blood to kick-start the process.

Here is where things start to get a little more complicated. To try to keep this simple, I'm going to break this down into six short parts.

1. Water
2. How your body gets glucose
3. Insulin and Fat Metabolism
4. Sugar
5. Feeds
6. Absorption, Osmolality, Glycemic Rate, Proteins
7. Actually feeding

Water

Our bodies require 2 things to sustain functionality: water and glucose. It is nice to have vitamins and minerals, but over a day or two, as long as you aren't sweating (which would mean replacing salt and possibly a very small amount of potassium), you really just need water and a way to get glucose.

When we do athletic things, we require more water. This is for two reasons—first, we sweat to keep cool. Second, we expel water vapor as a byproduct of mitochondrial respiration. Ultra-marathon cold-water swimmers don't need nearly as much water as a runner would need. We don't sweat much in the cold-water. At the same time, though, we do a lot of work (including keeping warm). Most people seem to drink about 6-14 oz (150-350ml) of liquid every hour (roughly the volume of a 12 oz can of soda)...some a little more and some a little less, but it doesn't seem to vary much from swimmer to swimmer, at least among people I know.

Drinking too much at once can have a hugely negative impact on a swim, as demonstrated by both my Catalina and my North Channel swims.

In the water, even when it is rough, it isn't too hard to down that much or more in 30 seconds. Once trick is not drinking that much, even when you are thirsty. It is better to take it in over time (if you're short, add an extra ounce per feed, not 6 extra ounces all at once).

Warm is far better than cold in cold water. If you are training, you often carry it with you (tucked into your suit), which means it will be cold. On the other hand, if you are doing a long event (and have a boat with you), you can usually get it warm. Body temperature is about 100F, but warmer is better. About 120-130F (50-55C) is ideal. Much warmer and it will be hard to drink. Hot (tea or coffee temp, 175-190F (80-90C) will scald the swimmer's mouth and very little will actually be swallowed (and can end a swim). Also, it is important to not get salt water into the feeds. The crew should use a fresh bottle every time.

How Your Body Gets Glucose

Your body needs glucose to keep going. Both your brain and your muscles. It is kind of important—like air and water. Because it is so important, your body has evolved ways to get glucose.

First, muscles and the blood have glucose in them ready to use. Not a ton, but enough for a burst of energy.

Second, the liver also stores glycogen. Glycogen is a very long chained carbohydrate that can be quickly broken down into lots of glucose. Think of glycogen as a slightly more complex version of sugar, that can be accessed almost immediately. Liver glycogen only lasts so long though—usually 2-3 hours without supplement in a trained endurance athlete.

Third, candy, gu, gels, soda, Snapple, honey, and anything else sweet or starchy (potatoes, rice, etc.) convert almost immediately into glucose when they get to our gut. We crave sugar because of a complex evolutionary mechanism in our brains that causes us to feel elation when we taste it. This is the same dopamine that is key to addiction.

Fourth, and perhaps most important for anything over marathon distance, is fat. Relatively fit people carry tens of thousands of calories of fat around. This can also be accessed during exercise, although your body has to be convinced that it is starving or that something similar is happening. Fat can be thought of as a fatty acid with a string of glucoses molecules attached to it. You have fat around your core, subcutaneous fat under the skin, and intra-muscular fat in and around your muscles. This is the absolute best source of energy for long endurance activities because of its density, but there are a few challenges to getting at it (as we'll discuss below).

Protein can be metabolized as well, but it is metabolically expensive to do so. Dietary protein can be burned, but neither quickly nor especially efficiently. When you are starving (literally, not figuratively) and also when you exercise, your body will begin to catabolize muscle (eat itself), burning muscle for fuel.

Finally, fat in your stomach can be turned into glucose also, but it is a longer process because ingested fat has to be metabolized before it can be taken up by the muscles.

It is worth noting, that pretty much all of these methods are in use in your body at any given time. The real trick is to figure out how to make your body favor the most efficient ones. Specifically, in an endurance event, you can only rely upon your glycogen and ingested glucose for so long. The key is getting to the fat stores which is super-efficient storage of glucose that will last for a very long time.

The big trick in all endurance sports is to deliver plenty of glucose to your muscles for as long a period as possible, without interruption.

Insulin and Fat Metabolism

It seems simple. Why don't we eat lots of carbs, or start burning fat? One thing that complicates things is insulin. Our bodies are regulated by hormones. It is a constant balancing act between hormones that buffer each other. When blood glucose levels rise, insulin is released from the pancreas (its alter-ego is glucagon). Insulin causes cells to take up glucose and instead of releasing fat for use by the muscles, it causes both adipose tissue (fat) and the liver to capture glucose, building fat and liver glycogen.

Fortunately, when we exercise, our bodies become hungry for glucose, and the release of insulin is somewhat repressed. We can take in a little sugar while exercising, without causing this insulin spike.

For a 50-mile run, or an ironman triathlon (assuming both would take about 8 hours), this strategy of eating carbs to supplement glycogen can often work (although not always). Non-endurance athletes seem to hit the wall at about 6 hours. Endurance athletes often hit it at closer to 8 hours. For longer events (in any sport), more carbs just don't do it. If you hit the wall, there are a couple of issues. One is that you slow way down, for 5-30 minutes usually, but sometimes longer. Not a good thing in a race, but even worse in cold-water. The second thing is that your brain doesn't get the glucose that it needs. Even if you might otherwise get through it, your mind will have a tough fight with your brain, which is using its natural instinct to protect itself and you.

In the past 5 years, a new strategy (theory) has come into fashion. That is, train to start burning fat as early as possible. The idea is that everyone will eventually bonk. After a bonk comes a recovery, and during that recovery the body switches to burning fat as the primary energy source.

There aren't a lot of people who do heavy endurance events that last longer than 6-8 hours in any sport (possibly because there is no money in these sports), but there has been little research to date. Also, if the theory is correct, it seems unlikely that there would be any products to be sold.

The theory (which seems to be working well for me), is that you minimize carbs outside of training, and that you train on an empty stomach for anything under 2 hours—no carbs. Most training for these ultra endurance events should be LSD (long smooth distance), pushing yourself to the highest level you can sustain without carbs.

There can be fast days and lifting (depending on training needs), but the focus is LSD on an empty stomach. Longer training swims (over 2 hours) are done with a small amount of slow digesting carbs. The theory is that this allows the body to switch over slowly to burning fat without ever hitting the wall.

The big problem with hitting the wall is that burning fat (ironically) requires glucose as a part of the metabolic process. If you hit the wall, you by definition have low blood glucose, but you need to deplete your glucose before your body starts shifting to burning fat as its primary source.

The 5-30 minutes that you have the piano on your back is the time when most of that tiny amount of glucose is being used by your brain, and whatever is left is being used to metabolize fat. At a certain point, you gain enough glucose from the fat that has been converted, and over a few minutes, as your blood glucose level begins to rise, you start to feel better.

If you can make this metabolic switch early and slowly, you completely avoid the bonk. Also, when you switch slowly, you don't lose core temperature because you are still able to generate heat.

I should point out that while this makes incredible sense to me, I have seen no good science on it yet. I've looked. There may be a study out there that is good, but given all the variables, there would have to be quite a bit of evidence to prove it works. I only have my own results, which are more good than not.

I've read a few articles and a couple of books that advocate this for endurance events, but the science behind them is thin. That said, the existing science does seem to support the theory. At least there doesn't seem to be any reason that it wouldn't work.

One thing that complicates getting good science is that a lot of people subscribe to the theory of supplementing with carbs, using liquid feeds. They train hard, and for swims of less than 90 minutes, train with only water. As they get in better shape, they start taking on fewer and fewer carbs. Generally, a lot of these people also have specialized diets. Many stay away from all refined foods (and have a lower carb diet as a result). They've achieved similar results (apparently starting to burn fat early in their events) unintentionally using a hybrid approach with similar success. It begs the question, are they successful in spite of the "cheating" or is a more moderate approach actually a better way of doing it?

Regardless, it is clear that every person's feeding strategy will need to be custom to them. Experiment. Have lots of choices on the boat, even if you think you know what you are going to do.

Sugar

Carbs are carbs are carbs. Except that a lot of people don't agree with this.

There are two schools of thought—simple sugars are best, and complex sugars are best. I subscribe to the first group, although with many caveats, but I wouldn't claim to know that simple is better, and there are many variations of both ways of doing it. Try many different ways, and have backup feeds on the boat (and not just all carbs and sugars). Not only are feeds different from swimmer to swimmer, sometimes it is different from swim to swim for a given swimmer. What follows is a discussion, not necessarily conclusions or advice.

For the purposes of this discussion, we're going to consider three kinds of sugar: monosaccharides (glucose, fructose), disaccharides (sucrose/table sugar), and polysaccharides (all other starches, including maltose/maltodextrin, starch from rice, wheat, corn and potatoes, and other carbs like super-starch). High fructose corn sweetener is something between a monosaccharide and a disaccharide, but we'll consider it a disaccharide for the purposes of this discussion.

Glucose is what our muscles and brains need, but any saccharide will work—our bodies convert all saccharides to glucose almost immediately. They all have roughly 4 calories/gram, and they are all carbohydrates (carbs).

There is some evidence (although it is quite thin) that different kinds of sugars are digested differently. For example, fructose seems to shoot straight to the liver according to most studies. Some studies likewise suggests that high fructose corn syrup causes fat to collect around the liver, which is one of the markers of metabolic syndrome and is often tied to obesity and any other diseases related to morbidity.

Some athletes believe that monosaccharides and disaccharides are best because they go straight to the muscles. The issue here is that they can also cause an insulin spike (especially after repeated feeds) which can in turn cause a drop in blood sugar.

Others believe that polysaccharides are better because they digest over a period of time. They can be used to deliver a constant stream of energy over 30 minutes (a normal feed cycle). The science on this is thin (and sponsored), and likewise the drinks can feel heavy.

There are a wide variety of gels and other delivery mechanisms that make them easier to eat, less heavy, or might slow down (or speed up) the absorption rate. These include protein and super-starch. All saccharides deliver similar amounts of energy to the body per gram, so much of the conversation is going to be around absorption, and will be intrinsically tied to liquid.

Regarding diet outside of the water, there seems to be some evidence that artificial sweeteners are tied to obesity. These studies are far more suspect (because fat people are always dieting; correlation here may not equal causation). It is clear that sweets cause the brain to want more sweets. NutraSweet is very sweet (much more so than sugar), as is Splenda. The jury is out on whether Stevia has the same effect as these other sweeteners seem to, but it is likely that they all have an effect on the brain, even if they have no calories.

Alcohol sugars (there are many including mannitol, maltitol, and sorbitol) are poison for me. I have no scientific evidence that they are bad, but as far as fake sugars go, all alcohol sugars make me sick (literally). Some diabetics seem to not have a problem with alcohol sugars, but it seems likely that they work on our brains the same way as sugar does. I can't speak to the science behind whether they are not bad for you, but I try very hard to stay away from them simply because they make me feel horrible.

Out of the water, having a lot of carbohydrates of any type seems to be generally a bad idea. The scientific evidence around all of these statements is relatively thin (thinner than was the proof that fat was bad when we were kids), but we seem to be getting healthier as a nation as we cut out carbs. I'd bet there will be good science on this in a decade, but we have to actually make sure there is good science behind these theories. I don't mind being an early adopter and experimenting with my body, but I realize that I am doing so as I wait for better science.

One other thing, personally, I've concluded for me that I want food that is as processed as possible when I'm swimming, and I want to stay away from processed food as much as possible outside of the water.

Feeds

How does diet affect our choices of what to take in for a long swim?

Many people including Freda Streeter advocate Maxim. It is a favorite of more English Channel swimmers (probably largely because of Freda) than any other drink. Others like CarboPro, Hammer, or will make their own drinks using either maltodextrin or a mixture of maltodextrin and other sugars. There is a school of thought that says that you should mix different kinds of carbs to create different pathways to digest the sugars, getting the longest lasting energy from each feed without a spike in insulin. There are others who believe that the more simple the sugar, the better (I tend toward this school of thought).

There is also a new-ish drink called UCAN (Generation UCAN Superstarch). This was originally formulated to be a slow release long chain polysaccharide for young children who were having trouble feeding. Because it is relatively dense and slow release, according to the manufacturer it has properties that prevent the insulin response, also requiring fewer feeds. Some of the more accomplished swimmers I know think it is great. Others think it is just expensive with no additional benefits over any of the other complex carb or plain sugar drinks (I agree).

Other swimmers (and runners) swear by a variety of drinks including coconut water (sugar water, really), Gatorade (processed high-fructose corn syrup), Snapple Peach Ice Tea and Lipton sweetened tea powder (I use these, and they have caffeine), apple juice, grape juice, Kool-aide. A few drink flat coke (caffeine and high fructose corn syrup). Many mix the above drinks together or have different drinks at different feeds. I would not recommend anything that has a strong flavor. They are too acidic and will eventually upset your stomach and burn your throat. Weak tea seems to be an alternative that many like, although it can turn your stomach acidic as well. Most drink warmed drinks. Warming UCAN and some of the other drinks just makes a gloopy mess. Most swimmers do not drink the drinks full strength, although many will do a few extra strength drinks (up to full strength) when they feel their energy is fading, especially toward the end of a swim.

Some swimmers leave this to their crew entirely (not me). The crews tend to decide what to feed based on a feeding schedule and vary from it mainly based on stroke count. A slowing stroke count often indicates dropping glucose levels.

Personally, I drink sweetened, diluted iced tea, warmed. I get the powdered mix or drink Peach Snapple. I drink to thirst, usually about 4-7 oz., about 2 of every 3 stops, which land about every 30 minutes. Some stops I drink water (I drink to thirst). I mix it about 40-50% strength, and I like it warm for tougher (colder, longer) swims. I don't take my first drink until at least 60 minutes in.

The Lipton (and the Peach Snapple, which I also like but can't get in many countries) also has a small amount of caffeine. I drink decaf coffee on land during the week. I try to have limit my caffeine to 2-3x what I'd usually have in an average day, which seems about right (decaf does have some caffeine). I also keep a few packets of Gu or one of the other gels that have some caffeine in them as well (25mg, 50mg, or 100mg) in case I'm flagging. A little caffeine is a nice boost in the last third of a hard swim.

I've tried all the other drinks, and don't really have a problem with any of them (except the UCAN that doesn't heat well). Mark Allen (a champion triathlete and coach) advocates simple sugar based drinks. I tend to agree. Save your money. I can't say don't use the others. They seem to work well for some people, but try a wide variety on longer swims, then choose one and get very used to it.

One thing that is important: much more important for swimmers. Choose something that will taste okay coming back up. It should be something very low in acid (and flavor). Throwing up in the water is a part of long distance swimming for most people. If you don't get seasick at some point, you are very lucky. I am one of the few people I know who doesn't ever throw up, although I do sometimes burp up. Also, everyone eventually has a bad feed day. Throwing up usually makes things a little better. Even if you don't throw up, you burp up when you are horizontal. Like I said, make sure it will taste okay coming back up. It is for this reason that experienced people (especially those who drink the maltodextrin drinks) bring lightly flavored fruit drinks (Kool-aide for example) as well as just plain water.

There are a lot of things people feed with. For 8 hours or less, you could have only drinks, or drinks and gels. Longer swims require some solid food. If you don't have any, your stomach will start to bother you. Also, solid food makes you feel human in the water, and gives you something to look forward to.

First, take NSAIDs. They are perfectly legal, like caffeine. Learn from me, though—DON'T EVER CRUSH THEM. I usually have a couple before an event, a couple mid-swim, and maybe a couple toward the end or after, depending on how rough and long it is. The NSAIDs help just with general soreness through the swim, but also, if it is rough, they help with my neck, which always gets sore in chop. Also, the chafing doesn't bother me quite as much when I've had a couple of Advil. I usually go with Ibuprofen, but Acetaminophen is fine, too. Aspirin has too much acid in it, but I always carry some. It is the one that I can chew to get immediate results if I have a headache after. Also Naproxen Sodium (Aleve) often works well, too.

A lot of people like smoothies. The people that like them seem to be the ones that make their own. Some of the ingredients I've seen include coconut water, almonds, avocado, coconut oil, fruit, and other natural ingredients. Remember, too much acid is a bad thing.

Smoothies have never worked for me…too much acid, too much fiber, too much glop. Personally, I think drinking drinks and eating solids is probably the better plan, at least for me, but again, everyone will have something that works best for them.

You always need to think about feeding fast. I shoot for 30 second drinks, and sub-1-minute if I'm eating (or doing both). The problem is that I like the company. Swimming for 30 minutes without talking to anyone can drive you nuts. I am realistically probably more like 30-60 seconds for most feeds. If you're wondering why so short, just multiply 1 extra minute by 20+ feeds…you don't want to be swimming that much longer. For longer and colder swims, discipline is incredibly important. If you are doing Gibraltar in good conditions, by all means— take in the view, enjoy the swim, and stop for a minute or two. But in colder water, rougher seas, or poor conditions, keep stops as short as possible. Thirty seconds should be the goal.

I'm listing a lot of possible feeds below, with some comments from my personal experience and what I've heard.

Drinks

- Lipton Peach Tea, powdered (I use this, but it is too acidic, water it down)
- Snapple (I use this, but can't get it everywhere, water it down)
- Maxim
- Hammer
- CarboPro
- Fruit Juice—apple, grape, citrus (I find citrus burns my throat on longer swims)
- Kool-Aide
- Flat Coke
- Gatorade
- UCAN Superstarch
- Coconut water
- Homemade maltodextrin drink (usually mixed with fruit juice of some sort)

Packets and Gels

- Cliff (90-100+ calories)
- Hammer (90-100+ calories)
- Gu (90-100+ calories)
- Gu blocks and Gu Shot gels (my favorite) (90 calories)
- Stinger gels (more calories per pack!) (160 calories)
- There are others, too, some with protein or caffeine

Bars

- Power Crunch (this is what I use, they have 14g protein, 9-10g carbs, 14 g fat) (~225 calories)
- Cliff Bars (too hard to chew); Granola Bars (takes too long to eat, too dry, will hurt your throat). Need soft.

Other Foods

- Yogurt (I use this for longer swims, maybe 5-6 total at about 8g protein/8g carbs)
- M&Ms late in the swim (this sounds great, but too much sugar for me)
- Canned peaches and their juice late in the swim (too much acid and sugar for me)
- Cheese (tastes very good, but only once or twice, and only late in a swim)
- Avocado (no thanks)
- Almond Butter (comes in packets, better after a swim)
- Bananas (they seem ideal for most people, but I personally don't like bananas)
- Coconut, ground (haven't tried, but suspect too much fiber—just doesn't sound appetizing)
- Coconut oil (haven't tried, but suspect too much fat)
- Amino acids (runners and cyclists use them, but I haven't tried them)
- Scrambled Eggs, with a little butter, (if there's a stove, it was very good on one swim!)
- Antacid (good to have just in case)
- Ground up Chicken with salt in a shake (no thanks, the idea makes me gag)
- Sardines (even worse than chicken)
- Oatmeal (a good idea, would likely taste very good)

I always bring along some gel packets in my suit. In rough water, I can always eat them quickly, even if I can't get close to the boat. The feed is fast, and the new ones even have a "catch" to save the top when you pull it off so you don't litter. They are also easy to handle. Many of them have small amounts of caffeine. Do make sure you don't have too much caffeine. There are a lot of variations on chocolate, which is good because none of my other food is chocolate, and although it gives me a little heartburn sometimes, chocolate anything always tastes good. Be sure to bring both your favorites, and a wide variety of others.

With gels, you will have a few choices to make (and many options to choose from):

- Caffeine (none, 25mg, 50mg, 100mg)
- Calories (90-160)
- Fruit, Chocolate or other flavor
- Whether the top is caught when torn off
- Protein supplement

I don't think there is much reason to think about the type of sugar in gels or cubes/blocks. They are all designed to absorb fast, and none have a ton of calories. Taste is probably the most important factor, and don't try to taste them when you are in the store. They taste very different when you're swimming.

As far as bars go, I like PowerCrunch bars. They taste best to me, and I can eat them reasonably fast (about 2 minutes). The protein/fat/carb mix is just right for me, as is the number of calories.

There are lots of good reasons for yogurt (see next sections), but the challenge is eating it in the water. In the US we can get tubes. Siggi's are great (8g protein, 8g carbs). Problem is that tubes don't exist outside the US.

Whatever you do, be sure to bring some solid food for later in the swim. Candy, cakes, fruit bowls (peaches!), anything that will put something semi-solid into your stomach, and that you will welcome. It is as important to look forward to it, as it is for nutrition.

Absorption, Osmolality, Glycemic Rate, Proteins

There is a small amount of literature about feeds in endurance events. Most of it is anecdotal, and most of it is around ultra-marathon runs (50k-100mi+). There is very little on longer runs, and nothing that I know of on swimming.

The little bit that there is suggests that a few topics are of special importance.

First, absorption. How many calories can we reasonably absorb in an hour without feeling sick? This question assumes insulin is not an issue (which you absolutely cannot assume), but in a fantasy endurance kingdom far, far away where insulin only kicked in when you wanted it to, how many calories of sugar could you reasonably process in an hour without causing your stomach to be upset?

The number than a few people have come up with is 450 calories per hour (possibly 10-20% more with training). I've not seen anything that supports that number, but personally, it just about matches with my experience. I could take in more (even as much as 800+ calories between two feedings), but I couldn't sustain more than about 500 calories per hour without starting to either feel sick or really slow down.

Second osmolality. How much water goes to your gut when you eat? There are a lot of medical studies around this, and most say that there are differences between carbs, proteins, and fats. Others suggest that certain products allow you to ingest more of their product without requiring your gut to pull in water to digest it, but there is little good evidence around these assertions (and most of the studies are sponsored). This is an important factor in deciding what to eat.

Too much of a solid (or even a liquid with dissolved or partially dissolved particles) could cause a lot of gastric distress, and could cause your blood glucose level to drop. This is an important factor. Likewise, how much water you can take in and continue exercising is very important as well. Too much and you end up with either a brick in your stomach, or a sloshing mess that takes a lot of time to absorb.

In endurance events, salt is also a big deal. In rough water, it is possible for a less-experienced open-water swimmer to swallow as much as a liter of water on a long swim. That much water is pretty miserable, but all that salt can mess up your digestion, too. Freda Streeter wisely suggests dumping your feed if it gets water in it. Very smart advice.

Third, is glycemic rate. How fast does what you ate go to the blood as glucose? Too fast can cause an insulin rush. But this has to be balanced with digestion. If a feed pulls water into the stomach to digest it, it could cause a lot of gastric problems which could lead to a far lower blood-glucose level.

The fourth factor is highly related. How do fat and protein affect the three factors above? If you can slow down digestions just a bit (and maybe have something more than just sugar and water in your stomach, you might improve the delivery of sugar to the muscles.

Finally, at what point do you need something in your stomach—something solid? What should it be?

If you take in enough straight sugar, your blood sugar will spike causing an insulin rush. No two ways about it. Also, if you take in a lot of water, the sugar will likely enter the blood stream more quickly, unless your stomach stops cooperating for any of a variety of reasons. In the real world, fiber slows down absorption, as do protein and fat. A channel, though, is not the real world. Too much of any of these could cause gastric distress.

There are a lot of questions, and although there are some answers and advice here (both scientific and anecdotal), the best advice you'll get in this book is to experiment.

Fiber is not a realistic option. It causes a great deal of work to be done. If you've ever swum after having a big salad or large plate of raw veggies, you never want to do it again.

Fat is not easy to digest, and neither is protein. But both have the effect of slowing carbohydrate absorption. If you are feeding every 30 minutes, getting your carbs to last 30 minutes is a great thing. If you can take in a small amount of protein and/or fat, you don't have to experiment with some expensive laboratory manufactured starch. The questions are, how do you best get it, and how much is the right amount? It likely isn't a lot, and it probably isn't something that should be sustained through a long swim.

I can only speak from experience and what others have told me, but over an hour it seems like having 10g of protein and 10g of fat, per every 30g of carbs is a maximum buffer that works well in any given hour. This shouldn't be done more than a few times in a 10-hour swim.

I've also noticed that when I ask the "mixers" and "shake people" what they use, in my head it seems like they are doing shakes with roughly those amounts. It is hard because what they say may or may not be what they actually ate, they may not have eaten all of it, and I may or may not be using good numbers in my estimates of what they are taking in. It would seem, though, that by trial and error, they're getting to about the same place as I am.

I've tried a few things that have not worked. Mostly protein does not work. Protein drinks do not work (don't heat up, and don't digest well). A lot of fat does not work (some is ok). A lot of solid food does not work (a little does). Meat of any kind doesn't work (tried jerky, tried chicken, even tried bacon). Milk does not work (although yogurt and cottage cheese seem to, they are just hard to feed on).

Having too much sugar early causes a spike. Too much protein early causes a brick in the stomach. The solution: Don't eat much at the beginning. The last half hour before and the first hour of the swim, don't eat anything. That said, don't start with low blood sugar. If you're hungry, it is probably best to have something light. Don't eat if you aren't hungry or drink if you aren't thirsty. Also, eat and drink less than you want. If you are really hungry or thirsty, you'll likely drink far more than you can effectively process. On some swims, as we've seen, this can really hurt you.

One other thing—no matter what anyone says, alcohol does not work. I've seen the effects first hand. For a big guy, a shot of Jameson's or a half a beer might not appear to have a huge negative impact, but it surely doesn't help. It can be outright dangerous, and it will have a negative impact. It is just stupid.

While cheese and scrambled eggs have both worked well when I've had them, I suspect that they did because my balance was off (or maybe I just needed something solid).

Sometimes having water or nothing at all is really what you need: no carbs (or even food) on some feeds. Sometimes having nothing is the right call.

While more and more people are choosing to supplement with protein and fat, there are still some people who just stick with what has worked for them in the past—Maxim, CarboPro or one of the other complex carb drinks. I would never judge their decisions. What works for one person might not work for another.

The smartest people who read this will look at everything in here and glean some knowledge about how the body probably digests food and fuels itself. But with that knowledge (that should be taken with a grain of salt, figuratively, not literally), this should be a starting point in determining what is right for each individual person. There is no single right recipe, at least not that anyone knows about now. It is all about learning what you can, and using trial and error until you find something that you can practice with, and get your body used to.

Actually Feeding

Eating food while exercising is tough. Just think of running a 10k: You don't really eat. For good reason, too. It would make you want to throw up and probably help you decide to walk. Probably no ham sandwiches on a marathon either. But in ultra-marathon runs (50km-100mi), they actually eat. Now, they also slow down for a few minutes, which isn't possible in cold-water, but the most successful ultra runners actually eat real food.

They are ahead of us in some ways, but we can't always just copy what they do. Little PB&J sandwiches taste awfully salty and mushy in open water. Also, it is hard to breath when you are chewing, especially when it is choppy. Peanut butter can taste incredible, but it is also slow to eat. Solid food also doesn't feel so good coming back up. Finally, solid food means solid waste. It isn't the worst thing in the world, but swimmers try to avoid that 3-minute delay for a whole variety of reasons.

Speed and getting as much of the feed to your stomach are the first two goals. After that warm is usually better than cold, and obviously not taking in any salt water is important. Another consideration is making it easy for the crew.

Get good bottles. Try them from a boat in practice swims. A drinking hole of about 1" (a little over 2cm) is best. Big enough to guzzle fast without getting too much air, and small enough that waves crashing over you won't contaminate your drink with salt water.

It doesn't matter too much if my bottles have rings on them, but it makes it a little easier. I always bring duct tape and brightly-colored light nylon rope. If it is calm, you can just throw the bottles back and forth, but in rougher water, it isn't possible. You want a rope on the bottle so it can be retrieved easily.

I usually have a feeding pole with clothespins on the end. Clothes pins are very good for getting a bar or yogurt or packet out to me from the deck of the boat. Apple pickers (the types with nets at the end) can also be good for passing food.

Some people always want kayakers. They are nice to have, but I'd rather have my crew warm on the boat. On a rough swim I don't want to have to worry about them, too, unless kayaks are absolutely necessary.

A white board is a good thing. The swimmer can't communicate back but it is very good for signaling and giving the swimmer information and messages. Know what you want to know and not know, and communicate that to your crew before the swim.

Be sure you can get into your feed. If the wrapper is too tough to open, it will take too long. Make sure that your crew pre-opens everything including bottles, wrappers, even Gu. It is amazing how hard it can be to open a Gu when you can't really feel much with your hands.

If you are going to carry stuff in your suit, bring a zip-lock bag with a slider top. It will keep your feed on your ass (better than between your legs). Also, wrappers tend to scratch a little— better in a Ziploc. I try hard to not ever litter. Sometimes you'll lose something. Don't worry about it, it does happen. But try. Pick up 5 pieces of trash during training swims for every one you drop, and you'll feel a lot better, too.

I try to pre-mix everything and I give clear instructions (even write them down) for my feeds. Personally, I direct my feeds. Some people have their crew direct their feeds. That is a personal decision, but I like to be in control of my swim. For others, it is one less thing to think about. I can see both sides. Regardless, your crew needs to taste every bottle before it goes to you—salt water in a feed can make you very sick, and too much or too little sugar can really throw you off.

Making sure feeds taste good is important. The psychological battle is half of everything. A little candy or treat at a milestone (10 miles or 8 hours, for example) can be very smart.

You don't know what you will want when you hit that low point. Bring a variety of things. You look forward to feeds. Physiologically, the down points have more to do with brain chemicals that are trying to protect your body than with whether your muscles can keep going (they usually can). The challenge is that you need to control your brain.

Everyone knows that exercise produces endorphins. Likewise, anyone who swims in cold-water knows that sunlight makes a huge difference. There is very little actual warming from the sun when you're mostly submerged. In fact, if it did warm the skin on your back, you'd be in quite a bit of trouble given that your vascular system would begin to ease the shunting effect which would quickly flood your core with very cold blood (this doesn't happen). It is something else—serotonin. The sun hits your skin, and your body releases serotonin. It makes you happy.

Now, no amount of serotonin or endorphins will make up for the pain you are feeling from the cold, but if you generally have shunted blood well and have your core temperature and the pain under control, a little of these hormones can make an otherwise tough swim an almost nice experience. Note, I said almost, and I didn't say warm or easy. It might just make things a little better.

Dopamine is another brain chemical that everyone knows. Good drugs, alcohol, sex, and sugar all trigger the release of dopamine. A funny thing, though, it isn't just the release of dopamine, but also the lack of reuptake of it that creates happiness in the brain. Sugar (and things that taste good) as well as caffeine can give you a temporary boost in dopamine (sugar lasts minutes, caffeine has a smaller but longer effect).

Cortisol imbalance is an enemy in training. Excess dopamine, overtraining, stress (like at work or home), lack of sleep, alcohol, stress (physical), can all cause a cortisol imbalance. An imbalance will suppress dopamine and generally will lead to lethargy, being in a depressed state, and poor performance. Cortisol is not so much a problem during a performance—your body is too busy. But it can have a horrible effect if you go into a swim lacking training because you've been depressed or even just not motivated. Worse, if you are in an imbalanced state going into a swim, your attitude will start at a far lower point. Thoughts of defeat are hard enough to keep out without having a cortisol imbalance. Be extremely conscious of your cortisol balance.

Fixing a cortisol problem can be hard or easy. Often it is just a matter of getting more sleep. Sleep helps with overtraining, lack of sleep, stress and many other factors. Sleep alone won't fix injuries, but it can help. Getting rid of the cause is also key. Alcohol, caffeine, stress at work/home, or other factors will continue to weigh you down until you fix the root cause. In short, get rid of the alcohol, caffeine, stress, and probably the sugar, and cortisol will come back to balance.

Appendix B – Rankings and Big Swims

This sport is cold-water ultra-marathon swimming. It is not marathon swimming, but for contrast it is useful to see how marathon swimmers are ranked.

Rankings in marathon swimming (relatively short at 5k and 10k distances, in usually flat warmer water and good conditions) are pretty simple. The fastest person in a given race is the best.

Warm water swims are a different endeavor as is anything that involves touching a boat. Neither are a part of our sport. Wet suits are not allowed in this sport, unless you are just starting or not competing. These all make a swim easier.

Cold-water ultra-marathon swimming uses English Channel Rules or something similar, which can be summarized as simply no assistance of any kind. Rankings are determined by what you accomplish, not by speed of a particular swim, as even the same swim on two different days can be very hard to compare.

Like the 7 Summits, there are the Oceans7 swims. These aren't necessarily the hardest swims ever done, but they are a good starting point. The Oceans7 (a challenge made up by Steve Munatones) include, in descending order of difficulty:
1. The North Channel of the Irish Sea
2. The English Channel
3. The Santa Catalina Channel
4. The Molokai Straight (Molokai to Oahu, Hawaii)
5. The Cook Straight
6. Tsugura Straight (Sea of Japan)
7. The Straights of Gibraltar

These not necessarily the 7 hardest swims, but they are certainly among them. The English Channel ("the" iconic swim) is about 21 miles and is the yardstick by which swims are measured.

In this sport, "ranking" is determined by how many big swims you've done and the water temperature of those swims. To date, the Oceans7 has been completed by 6 people. This is a pretty elite group. Fewer than 100 people have done 3 or more (September 2016).

There are certainly some other swimmers who are active and should be counted despite not having completed many of the Oceans7 (or some like Allison Streeter and Kevin Murphy who should be at the very top because they have both done more than one TRIPLE CROSSING of the English Channel). In any case, the way to rank someone is by the number and difficulty of the swims they have completed.

In this sport, an incredible swimmer like Trent Grimsey (who holds the record for the fastest English Channel crossing) garners more respect because of his speed. He is fast and anyone that can do the English Channel that fast (even on a perfect day) is an incredible swimmer in our sport.

That said though, just as respected are those who finish taking a long time. There are people who have been in English Channel 3 times longer than Trent—now that commands respect. The water is cold, and it hurts to swim that long. Like swimming fast, the longer the swim (in terms of time), the more respect you get in this sport. It doesn't mean that you are fast, but it means that you endured, and this is an endurance sport.

Also, every swim is different. Two different days on any Channel or swim can be so completely different that they can't even be compared. When you combine these, it becomes difficult to use consider a person's time as a measure. It is for this reason that people are ranked simply by what they've done.

There are many ways to decide which swims are hardest, but generally, the list above (Oceans7) or the list below, a list of many of the hardest swims that have been done or attempted (that suffers from my subjective point of view) might be a starting point. Anyone with many of these swims should be considered elite in this sport, especially if many of those swims are near the top of the lists.

The 6 people who have done all of the Oceans7 swims, and those who have done the Farallons, Irish Sea, Isle of Wight, and Double and Triple Crossings of the English Channel are among the best in the sport. Another challenge is the Triple Crown (EC, Catalina, and MIMs around Manhattan). Finally, there is an exclusive group of swimmers who are members of the "24-Hour Club." Most people consider any swim not done according to "English Channel Rules" or a largely similar pre-published rule set to not be a valid swim in this sport.

Figuring out who is best among the top group begins to get tough at the highest ranks. Kevin Murphy and Allison Streeter would be names that would likely be the first to rise to the top of most people's rankings, but who comes next is good pub topic.

As far as swims go, the list below is quite incomplete (there are many more bodies of water out there). Hopefully someone will compile a better list. I've attempted to put them in rough order of difficulty, but this is hard. Any swim on any day can be far tougher than the stats might otherwise indicate.

My apologies for swims that I've left out or put in the wrong order. Distance is based on best information available, and temperature is the best estimate of the average temperature when most attempts are made. There are so many swims possible in the world, in lakes, across channels, between/around islands, and across bays. These are just a few that are often talked about.

1. Triple Crossing English Channel (63 miles/101km, rough, 60F/15.5C)
2. Isle of Wight (56 miles/90km, rough, winds, 60F/15.5C)
3. Farallons (30 miles/48km, rough, sharks, 58F/14.5C)
4. Double English Channel (42 miles/68km, rough, 60F/15.5C)
5. North Channel of the Irish Sea (21 miles/34km, rough, jellyfish, 54F/12C)
6. English Channel (21 miles/34km, rough, standard for cold-water ultra-marathons, 60F/15.5C)
7. Circumnavigation of Jersey (43 miles/69km, 64C)
8. SCAR (40 miles/64km over 4 days, freshwater, pool temp)
9. Straights of Magellan (4 miles/6km, rough, hard to arrange, 38-42F/3-5.5C)
10. Juan de Fuca (13.8 miles, 49F/9.5C but often colder)
11. Catalina (21 miles, 66F/18.5C)
12. Molokai (26-28 miles, 74F/23C)
13. Loch Ness (22 miles, 55F/12.5C but often much colder)
14. Sweden to Mariehamn, Finland (25 miles, 56F/13C)
15. Lake Erie (24 miles, windy, 68-76F/20-24C)
16. Bering Strait (shorter, but really cold—in the low 30s)
17. Lake Titicaca (26 miles/various longer and shorter routes, 12,000ft/4000m elevation, 56F/14C)
18. Lake George (32 miles, 78F/26C)
19. Lake St. Claire, MI (22 miles, 68F/20C)
20. Tahoe (21 miles, 6,000ft/2000m altitude, 68F/20C)
21. Cook Straight, NZ (18 miles, hard to hit shortest route, rough, 57-66F/14-19C)
22. Tsugura (12 miles, weather, rough, 65F)
23. Sandhammaren Sweden to Bornholm Island (23 miles, 63F)
24. MIMS (28 miles, but strong tidal assist, 60F+)
25. Gibraltar (8.8 miles, 68F/20C; can be rough; iconic swim)

Appendix C – Planning a Swim

You've been swimming for a few months, and you want to do something a little tougher. Not an organized swim, but a signature swim. What do you do?

First thing is that you need to decide where you are going to swim. This might sound like an easy thing, but it has to be hard enough to be worthwhile, yet something that is possible to do. First, measure the point-to-point distance on a map. You can use a site called www.freemaptools.com/measure-distance.htm. Remember that distance for a swim is determined by the shortest realistic route, not the actual route you might travel and not the route including the path the current may carry you on.

Next, you have to calculate tides. This is a lot harder than it might seem. You can get tides online, but you have to map out where you'll be, hour-by-hour, and what the tidal effect will be. For some swims, this isn't too difficult. For others, it can take many hours, and require you to change your plans. You also need to plan for a range of challenges that can change timing (more or less tide, faster or slower swimming, wind, chop). You need to have thought through what you will do if you are not going to make your goal (do you have a secondary goal?), if you exceed your goal (do you go further?), if you are swimming in place (how long will you keep going?), if you have boat traffic that requires you to hold.

Once you have a course (or maybe even before), you'll need to get people to help. This is always tricky. I always worry about asking people to spend 5-10 hours on a boat helping me. Many people love to do it, and want to help in such a fun endeavor. Others are happy to do it for money. Regardless of how you find people, you'll need at least a few. Fewer people can do a swim that is relatively easy for you. As you get longer and the swim becomes more challenging to you, you'll need more people. Here is a short list:

1. Kayaker—not always necessary, but often always nice to have; if you have kayakers and your swim is over 6 hours you should have 2 who alternate
2. Pilot—maybe a small motor boat or a big boat (depends on the swim). For a swim less than 5 hours, you can often do with just a kayak
3. Crew—over 10 hours often requires two people; less than 5 hours can sometimes be done by the pilot
4. Witness or Observer—if you want it to count somehow, then you'll need an observer or witness

For bigger (Channel) swims, you'll often have all of the above, plus more crew, a first mate, and sometimes even a cook and/or deck hand(s).

If you are crossing borders, you'll need to clear the swim with both governments. Often, you'll also need to notify the coast guard, too. The pilot should know where shipping lanes are, and will likely have something to say about the course you've chosen. Also, there are other factors that the pilot may consider.

Finding people you trust is hard. Good pilots are worth their weight in gold, and may ultimately determine your fate—not just the fate of your swim, but sometimes the fate of your life. Ditto for your crew. Don't expect your pilot to be bright or chipper, or even positive. That is your crew's job. Pick them wisely. For crew, it is all about attitude. Your kayakers are like your crew, but they also need to be able to kayak a long way. It isn't easy.

Your crew has three main jobs: feeding you, making sure you don't die, and helping you when you get back on the boat. It is your job to make sure that they can do all of these jobs. They should know what you might feed on, and they should be watching your stroke count. They should know when you are getting cold, if you need sugar, if you're getting tired, when you need encouragement, if you need a kick in the ass, and when you need to be pulled. They should know the signs of hypothermia, and know what you look like at various stages of getting cold. Pulling you too soon is bad. Pulling you too late means death. It is an important job. When you get back in the boat, you'll likely be in pretty bad shape, especially after a tough swim. They'll handle food, warm liquids, Tylenol/ibuprofen, mouthwash, getting dry, getting into clothes, taking care of chafing/sunburn, and helping you get on the boat if there's a problem (which is like helping a 200-pound fish on a boat).

The pilot will have a whole lot of safety stuff to worry about (I won't write about what I don't know about). Generally, though, you want to have a whistle (to get the swimmer's attention), a horn (to get the swimmer's attention fast), and radios (plural). The pilot may need navigation equipment. Before you leave, the pilot needs to notify vessel traffic and keep them informed throughout the swim, especially when you get out.

A Word about Witnesses and Observers

A witness is generally required for qualifying swims and any swims that are more than just for fun. If you want to say you did it, you need someone to say they were there (two people could each be there for half, as long as they overlap and even two people swimming together can vouch for each other). Your pilot can also be a witness.

For any major accomplishment, any first, any channel swim, or any record, you absolutely must have an observer (not just a witness). Where a witness could be a friend or fellow swimmer, an observer must have ALL of the following traits:

- The observer must have unimpeachable credentials (be a part of a swimming association, or well respected in the community)
- Have nothing to gain should you achieve your goal, and not be a part of your "team"
- Must be there the whole time, and awake, or have a second observer who takes over when the other sleeps
- Must keep a log that includes temperature, conditions, tidal information, progress, stroke counts, and observations at least hourly. Most do this at every feeding, and most take video and pictures at regular intervals.
- The observer must enforce a clear set of rules for the swim that can be confirmed. English Channel or MSF swimming rules are most often cited. Any exceptions must be clearly laid out in advance. This is both so that success can be measured, and also so that others can replicate the feat.

A swimmer recently claimed to have swum from Cuba to Florida. Her observer did not meet any of the above criteria. The person who was the observer was not credentialed or unimpeachable, and clearly had an affiliation with the swimmer (potentially even something to gain from her completing the swim), was not awake the whole time, did not keep a log the whole time, and did not have a clear set of rules before the swim began (and clearly allowed the rules that were described to the press to be violated). Without an observer, people began to question the veracity of the swim. Based on quite a bit of evidence, there are now few informed people in the ultra-marathon community who believe that she actually completed the swim as she said. Most believe that she was towed by the boat for more than 25 miles. While the swim was still an incredible feat of endurance (whether she cheated or not), it is not likely that she completed the swim honestly. This is a real shame. There aren't a lot of cheats in this sport, but there will always be some.

It is easy to make a swim unimpeachable. There are always many people in the community willing to help.

Appendix D – A Few Questions

These are questions that I've gotten many times over the years.

<u>What did you learn about yourself from your marathon swims?</u>

I learned that I can endure a lot more pain that I would have thought. I also learned that the water is always cold...you never really get used to getting in and cold-water is, well, cold. You learn to ignore the pain, but the water is still cold. You are still cold—your skin, your fingers, toes, hands, feet. It is the pain that you can just say no to...the pain from the cold, the sensation that you can't feel anything (you can still feel a little, and you have to work with that). You can still not just move, but you can actually control your muscles and even keep your form (or at least some of it). I've also learned that being tired and sore are just a perception that isn't always accurate. Your body can keep going if your mind simply tells it to—you can ignore what your nerves are telling you. You might not be going as fast, you might not get the time you'd expected, but if you just keep going, eventually the negative parts of your brain will realize that you actually are doing it. I don't think I'm so special. I just keep going sometimes when the smart part of my brain says to get out. Nothing a little ben-gay, a massage, food, and some good sleep won't fix.

<u>Why do you do marathon swims?</u>

For the adulation of the fans, the beautiful women who throw themselves at me, and the money.

I was never a great pool swimmer. I know great pool swimmers (Craig Marble was one), and I am not one. I could always keep up in workouts (the longer the workout, the better I got). I just wasn't all that fast. I couldn't even hold a candle to guys who swam the 500, 1000, and 1650 when I was at Cal. I was lucky the coach let me swim. In 1994, a friend brought me to swim in the Bay. It was eye opening. I still wasn't fast, but I could just keep going. My 1000 pace was the same as my 10-mile pace. And I loved it. Being in the water resets my mind. I'm a nicer person after I swim. More creative, too. The pool has some of the same effect (polo and the black line), but nothing clears my mind as much as swimming in open water. I've always loved the water, and doing long swims (as hard as they are) is the thing that makes me feel completely in my own mind.

<u>What do you think it takes to do a marathon swim?</u>

A marathon swim is officially 10km. Add cold-water to this, and you have a challenging event. It will take between 2.5 and 5 hours depending on your speed.

Let's say your New Year's resolution is to do a 10km swim in the summer. You start by having a reasonable stroke. It doesn't need to be perfect, but you need to not be hurting yourself. A 10km swim is about 9,000-18,000 strokes, so you need to make sure that you aren't damaging your shoulders or causing yourself unnecessary neck/back pain. Any coach in any masters program can help you get a passable stroke in as short as 1-3 months. By spring, your stroke should be sorted. Once you have your stroke down, start swimming farther. Ideally, you want to be in the water 4-5 days a week. If your swim is going to be in cold water, train in cold water. Either way, be in open water as often as possible. You need to learn to sight, you will likely lengthen your stroke, and you will need to learn to feed. Beyond 10km, most people would want to go without food and water.

Start by swimming a little. Do as much as you can (even if it is only 15 minutes). The next time you are out, swim 5 minutes farther. Do this each time, until you are up to an hour. Once you can do an hour, plan longer swims—90 minutes, 2 hours, 2.5 hours, 3 hours. Do a longer swim each week. This will build up your tolerance to the cold, your confidence, and also your endurance. Make a plan and stick to it. On longer swims, feed. Feed is different for every person...you'll need to experiment, and you don't want to do it during your event.

It is also a good idea to buddy up with someone who has done longer events. There are a ton of people with great experience willing to help at SERC. The open-water swimming community is one of helping others.

If you loved the 10km swim (whether done with just a boat from the club, or some sort of event), take on Gibraltar. At 8.8 miles, it is a very do-able swim. It just takes patience because registration is 1-2 years out.

<u>What do you wish you'd known before your first marathon swim (and what was that swim)?</u>

My first ultra-marathon swim (excluding the qualifier, which was 10 hours) was the English Channel. This answer is easy. I wish I'd known that I didn't need to gain so much weight. I gained about 50 lbs. for the swim. Skinny is not good in this sport, but I could have easily gained 15 lbs. instead. Not that gaining the weight wasn't a lot of fun, but I now realize that it wasn't something that was good for me.

What do you think about when you swim that long?

The best is when you're in the zone. You really don't think about anything. Your body is working the way it should, and you are relaxed and long in the water. It is a great place to be, a lot like meditation. A good swim will have a lot of this.

Unfortunately, not all of every swim is in this Zen-like state. Sometimes there is a song; that is the worst. Other times, you stress (Am I late? What if the tide turns? Am I swimming the right way?). Both of these are no good. The worst is stress about the swim. It is usually when my brain is not getting enough glucose. It is when negative thoughts burrow their way into my consciousness. Getting rid of these thoughts is hard. I say to myself, "This too shall pass," or simply think that the thought came from my brain. My mind is smarter and I'm going to choose to discard it like a bad dream. Having these tools is very important.

Slightly better for me is math. I get some set of numbers in my head, and work on them. Sometimes it is times, strokes, or tides, or work/money. It is just a way to occupy my mind…not the best, but better than stress or an earworm (song stuck in your head).

Sometimes in races (I don't do many, but there are some), I'll either think about where I am in the race relative to other people, or about strategy (when do I burst?). It does occupy your mind, and I have to remember to swim my own race. It isn't the worst thing, though. Sometimes it can give you just the push you need to have a great swim.

Next best is working out something challenging or hard. I get a lot of good thinking in when I'm swimming. This is far different than stress. It is actually thinking through bigger picture stuff and innovative ideas. Sometimes they are problems or issues, but more often they are good—like growth strategies (either personal or business). I like this. I get a lot of this thinking done when I'm training, but less on big swims. I think I'm just more focused by the time I get to the day of the swim. Also, worth noting: After I swim, I usually have a lot of clarity (hours after training, and in the days after an event). I figure out a lot at these times. It is when I plan my most diabolical and crazy schemes!

Just better than thinking about challenges and innovative ideas is being purely focused on stroke, breathing, heartrate, and mechanics. This usually precedes the Zen-like state, and is also very good. When I focus on swimming, I swim faster and more efficiently.

Sometimes it is a progression from the least good to the best (Zen-like state), but not always.

What stroke modifications should I make for swimming longer distances in open water?

Open-water swimming is just swimming and most of the things you learn in a pool are highly applicable here. At the same time, though, there are a few small things that are different from watching the black line.

First, an open-water stroke is longer. This is an endurance sport, not a speed sport. Efficiency is highly important. When you are going longer distances, you need to put more emphasis on the back part of the stroke rather than trying to gain the speed from the front part of the stroke. This isn't to say that having good form isn't still important (don't drop elbows and make sure you have a good catch), but put more energy into a long finish than a powerful catch. Long is key. Watch the 1500 free from the Beijing Olympics. The winner (Sun) has that long stroke (I have to pretend he didn't get caught doping).

Second, having a long stroke requires a good shoulder (and hip) roll. This is important for a variety of reasons, but rotation around your central axis is especially important when you are doing open-water swimming. Get someone to film you with your phone so you can see what you are doing.

Third, keep your head down. Just like in the pool. How is this different? Sighting. Many people sight forward every 4 or 8 strokes (like in water polo). This is not efficient. Do sight, but get good at swimming straight. Pick a target and swim to it without sighting at all. This will help you understand if you pull to one side.

Keeping your head down will keep your body position correct. This also puts less stress on your neck and shoulders. Every 20 or 40 (or even 80 strokes) is good. If you are in a large group of people, you can sight more initially, but when things thin out a little, get your head back down. If you can't sight forward, how do you know where you are going?

Fourth, sight when you breathe. Breathing every 3rd will give you a very good view of what is around you, and will allow you to triangulate to understand your position. This takes practice, as the information is imperfect. It usually is enough though, even in low light with foggy goggles. If you need to look forward, do 2 very low, very short looks to keep your body position as flat as possible. Two sights will give you a better ability to take in information and time to process it, then verify it on the second pass. It will be imperfect, but added to your side sighting, you can glean what you need. (Note: Personal admission: I usually breathe just to my strong side. I should breathe bilaterally.)

Finally, something Ranie Pearce planted in my head years ago. Have fun. Don't worry so much that your swim becomes work. This isn't work, it is play, and when it comes down to it, this is one of the best things in the world, done in one of the most beautiful places on the planet. Have fun.

Don't you worry about sharks?

When I'm talking about sharks, the story-line I've been using for years is that I'm more likely to win a Nobel prize than be bitten by a shark (which is technically true, but employs some statistical tricks). Not everyone has a shot at Nobel Prize or an Academy Award (also statistically more likely, as is being killed by lightning or winning the lottery). But neither does everyone swim in the ocean for hours on end where sharks are known to frequent.

I'm going to try to be a little more accurate. I did a little research. I'm scheduled to swim in Hawaii sometime in early March 2017, and I wanted to be accurate in accessing my chances with sharks. The following is all specific to Hawaii.

1. Oct-Dec is the period where there are the most attacks per person (based on number of attacks vs. number of people in the water in the state of Hawaii).
2. Tiger sharks are the real concern. Other sharks rarely attack unprovoked and usually do less damage when they do.
3. Statistically, spearfishing is the most likely to cause a shark attack (there are relatively few spear-fishermen, but a fair number of attacks on them). Being near fishing (bloody fish) is also highly correlated with attacks. Surfers are also attacked far more than swimmers (swimmers include SCUBA divers and snorkeling).
4. Most of the attacks are around Maui, and most of the currently tracked sharks are near Maui right now (near the shelf, where the water starts to get deep). All the other

islands have a far lower incidence of attacks. Maui vs. all the other islands is about 10 to 1.

5. There have only been 8 unprovoked shark attacks resulting in deaths in 35 years in Hawaii. 5.4m people swim/surf in Hawaii each year. A regular person in the water has roughly a 1 in a million chance of being killed in Hawaii if they are in the water.

6. If I assume that I'll be in the water 10x what most people are on a given trip to Hawaii (increasing my odds by a factor of 10), but that I'm not swimming anywhere near the Maui shelf (reducing my odds by a factor of 10), my chances of being killed are likely about the same as any other person in the water in Hawaii, statistically. Again about 1 in a million.

7. Randomly, no deaths have ever been recorded in March (in the last 35 years). This is not statistically significant given the small number of deaths. I hope to not be the first.

8. The odds of any member of the screen actors guild or those who produce movies (roughly 250,000 people) winning an Academy Award (50 given out each year) is about 1/5,000. If I were had an actor friend, she'd have a far better shot at winning an Academy Award than I would dying on a swim—by a factor of about 200 to 1.

Funny, I've never been worried about sharks. They don't really enter my mind at all. I've never seen one in the wild. I have seen dolphins and whales within a hundred yards of me swimming. I'll minimize my chances of being bitten in Hawaii (using a device on the kayak for sure, and maybe one on my ankle, too), but statistically I'm far more likely to be killed in a car accident (on the order of 1 in 10,000 this year, or 1 in 600 in my lifetime). I should be concentrating more on driving carefully to the boat and incidentially, not getting hit by the boat (which is the real danger in the water).

Appendix E – Day and Night

Many people don't like the idea of swimming in the Bay because you can't see below you. It isn't clear at all. You can't see more than about a foot. I know others who really don't like swimming where they can see the bottom.

Swimming in the dark is just a variation on the same theme. Above the water, the only way swimming in the dark is different is that you sight on lights instead of objects. Below the surface, you may have a little less visibility if the water is clear.

Granted the underwater views in Catalina, Hawaii, and Parts of the Pacific Northwest are incredible, but if you're in deep water, it doesn't make much difference. You can't see the bottom when it is deep even if the water is clear.

It is good to get used to swimming in the dark. It isn't a big deal.

Swimming in the Bay (and anywhere out in open water) is relaxing. There are great views from the water, and you always have to be wary of boats (and even other swimmers), but eventually that all falls away.

There are no cars or cell phones. There's no TV, no radio, no noise, except the sound of water. There's nothing to look at and nothing to see. You pop your head up every so often to navigate, but not too often. You want to stay efficient and raising your head is anything but efficient. Nothing to hear except the sloshing of the water. The only thing you can focus on is what is in your mind and what your body is doing. Eventually, you get to a Zen-like state where you are not thinking—where your mind is completely clear. It is this that allows me to think creatively. Sometimes my mind works through things while I'm swimming (without my intervention). Sometimes, the creative solutions come after a good swim.

At night, you get to this state faster. At first you think a lot about navigating. Your sight is far more limited and you have many fewer landmarks. Eventually, though, your brain situates you, and you get comfortable with a lesser degree of accuracy in where you are. You don't get lost, you just have less precision in your location.

Once you gain a comfort level with your location, it is very quickly quite quiet. I'd imagine, kind of like being in a sensory deprivation tank (although I've never been in one). There are lights (either from the boat or from the shore, depending on whether it is a training swim or a real swim). In Catalina, there was phosphorescence—illumination that is magical. Usually, though, it is just quiet.

As you swim, you exorcise all the demons. Bad thoughts seem to work their way out, and you start thinking about good things. This is especially true in the dark.

Night is colder. If not physically, then psychologically. The air and the surface water are usually colder, too, even if the surface water is only colder by a couple of degrees.

After a while you start thinking about warmth. Blankets, sleeping. But you have to fight that. It means hypothermia. How long is it until sunrise?

First light is nice, but it doesn't help much. It is sunlight that helps. It eventually makes a difference in surface water temperature, and also will surely warm your back a little once the sun is high enough. But when the sun rises or comes through the clouds, it is huge. You feel warmer. Your mood gets a boost. You can do anything. You will finish this.

I suspect this has something to do with serotonin. I don't know how it works, but when the sunlight hits you, everything gets just a little better.

Appendix F – What to Bring on a Swim

Here is a quick list of things to bring:

- 2 suits, 2 pairs of goggles, 2 silicon caps
- glow sticks and LED lights
- Sunblock and/or zinc oxide (diaper rash cream)
- Claritin, lidocaine, and steroid cream, epi pen, steroid pills (for jelly stings)
- ear plugs (if you use them)
- Lanolin and Vaseline or grease for chafing
- Tegaderm (for chafing)
- antacid
- NSAIDs
- Ice Chest (on cold swims put hot water in the bottom to keep drinks warm
- A Thermos full of hot water
- Drinks, extra bottles
- Feed
- Rope (thin, nylon), Duct tape, Clothes pins
- Feeding stick
- Razor (for guys to shave right before)
- Passport (if required)
- Spot Tracker, extra batteries
- Camera/Phone
- Warm clothes and towel (disposable if wearing grease)
- Water (a couple of gallons)
- Solid food (almond butter, nuts, or jerky) for after
- Food for the crew

A Few Pictures

Sue

Family in Italy

Annika, Ethan, Kylie

40053360R00148

Made in the USA
San Bernardino, CA
10 October 2016